⟨ **W9-DGK-191**

Education in America: A Dilemma in the 21ˢᵗ Century represents a detailed look at the double standard in public education that prepares minority children for failure. Jeffrey Dean Swain poses the question: why does this dual system of education exist fifty years after *Brown v. Board of Education*? Equal education does not result from integration but from access to equal resources.

Jeffrey Dean Swain demonstrates that minority children are most likely to receive the least experienced, least certified and most unmotivated teachers. Additionally, they are the unwitting victims of administrative policies that limit their chances for success. Minorities are the students most likely to be placed in special education and the least likely to be classified as gifted. He does not demand that public education be abandoned; rather, he challenges parents to recognize the disparity in learning opportunities and understand the consequences of failure.

His central theme is that we can be proactive in understanding the problems of education and in solving them. They are complex, but we must start by being honest about the condition of the system. He reminds the reader that different outcomes are built into the present education model. As America wrestles with its direction in the new millennium, it cannot exclude a re-examination of the public education system.

Finally, in the *Swain Doctrine of Education,* Jeffrey Dean Swain proposes ten things we can do to make public education better. His greatest desire is for America to live up to its promise of equality for all. He writes with the hope that others seek the same goal.

Education in America

ISBN: 0-9722175-1-7
LCCN: 2004096133

Cover designed by Mel-San Enterprises
P.O. Box 565504
Miami, Florida 33256-5504
1-800-624-6848

Contact the Author:
drswain@bellsouth.net

Printed in the USA by
Morris Publishing
3212 East highway 30
Kearney, NE 68847
1-800-650-7888

About the Author

Jeffrey Dean Swain is a *Phi Beta Kappa* graduate of Morehouse College, and he holds a Master of Science in Educational Leadership from Nova Southeastern University and a Juris Doctorate from the University of Miami School of Law. He previously published **Black and Still Here** and *A World of Color.*

Table of Contents

Dedications

This book is dedicated in the name of our Lord and Savior Jesus Christ to:

The late Rev. Prince Albert Swain, Sr. and Mrs. Frances Swain, my loving parents who remain dear to me. Joe Ann and Kia, two people who believe I am worth the trouble.

Rev. Abner L. Fortson, of Philadelphia, Pennsylvania, a man of God of the first order in whom the Spirit of God dwells richly. Sis. Lillian Fortson, God's example of quiet power.

Melvin and Dr. Sandra Billingslea, my unyielding friends and supporters.

Rev. Warren Clarke, my friend, who encourages good things in the Lord.

All good educators who love children and make dreams like mine come true – especially Mr. Howard Schutzman, Ms. Ellen Goodman, Ms. Ellen Heidt, Ms. Donella McIntee, Dr. Melvin Rahming and Dr. David Dorsey.

All children of all births to whom I wish God's speed in their life's endeavors.

All ancestors, black and beautiful, who were captured and tortured, died as slaves, held their tongues, fought and suffered humiliation but endured for me. As I was recently reminded by Dr. Asa Hilliard, *"If we forget our ancestors, we will die."*

Amor siempre.

Foreword

Jeffrey Dean Swain has reached the next level in his discussions on counteracting racial prejudice. In his pursuit of solutions to the problem of racism, he has gone to great lengths to study the issues and engage in dialogue on both local and national stages. His passion has always been to understand the African Diaspora and its affects on Africa's sons and daughters in their various corners of the world. Here, he turns his attention toward public education.

Looking back at his development as a thinker, he has always sought equality for the less fortunate. However, as adjunct professor of education and an administrator in the public school system, he has turned a love for learning into a passion for helping all children receive the same high quality of education he received. His goal is for all children to be treated fairly.

In *Black and Still Here* and *A World of Color*, his first two books, he explored the historical origins of race and its effects on the victims. He sees the African community as a worldwide family spread across continents whose separation has made them strangers. He wants to bridge those gaps. To do so, he believes unspoken issues must have their day.

In *Education in America : A Dilemma in the 21ˢᵗ Century*, he focuses on the different outcomes students experience in a two-tiered educational model that treats them differently according to their racial and ethnic backgrounds. Do not allow the title of the book to confuse you or lead you to believe that its content is narrow. On the contrary, it has broad implications for anyone who loves children and cares about education.

It has been enlightening to watch his development. Having worked with him from the conception of his first book, I can say he has evolved intellectually. *Jeffrey Dean Swain may be one of the best thinkers of our time.* I challenge you to engage yourself in this rich text and consider the information provided. You cannot read this book and be unchanged.

Jeffrey Dean Swain is not a mere social critic. He proffers *The Swain Doctrine of Education*, a well-conceived list of suggestions for how public education can be improved. His intentions are that all children get a chance.

Dr. Sandra Billingslea, President
Mel-San Enterprises, Inc.

Preface

In *Education in America*, I hope to highlight the crisis of America's dual system of education. As the country becomes more diverse, its students are having increasingly isolated educational experiences. Educational separation, coupled with housing segregation, means that white children and their minority counterparts will meet in college or in the workplace laden with misconceptions about one another, born out of the simple fact that they have had little or no prior contact.

The two groups are educated in a bifurcated public education system that places one group on the path to success and places the other group on the road to economic hardship. Why is the basic educational experience different at all? It should be relatively uniform. However, minority children languish in schools where uncertified and ineffective teachers and poverty hinder their chances for success; and parents are often indifferent, unavailable or frustrated.

An education system that ignores the problem of race, promotes a curriculum that denies the length and breath of racism's continued effects on people of the African Diaspora, and divides the population into increasingly rich and poor classes can only collapse under its own misdeeds. Americans tend to ignore racial issues. We who love children and love education must rail against losing children to mis-education.

My goal in writing this book is to question why the differences in the quality of education are so drastic and so persistent. I do not question our educational strategy for the sake of being a mere critic. Anyone can complain. I want to cajole, if not coerce, people into doing what's right. I owe every ounce of training I have received to people who cared about public education. This generation of children deserves our utmost.

I have been asked to soften the criticism. After some thought, I must say here that no one ever asks those who discriminate to mitigate their actions. When minorities are denied opportunities for advancement, given poor health care, denied community development and the deprived of the best educational experiences, no one tells their assailants to consider the injury. The worst mistake one can make in life is to be silent or compromising in the face of wrong.

I also care that children are being indoctrinated to fail. They are born with a desire to explore and create. They are not born believing in failure. Public education should not rob them of their unabashed enthusiasm for learning. Our present education system incrementally teaches minority children to have low expectations and to distrust and dislike education.

I could not stand before a just God knowing that black and minority children are being underserved and feel sure that I had used my time on earth wisely. As a Christian, I am obligated to fight wrong. As a believer in Christ, I am dedicated to recognizing low achievement as sin. As a Morehouse Man, I owe service to my community. As a son of the African Diaspora, I must honor the spirits of the ancestors who died for me to live.

Jeffrey Dean Swain, J.D.

Chapter One
The State of Things

Every time I decide to walk away from the issue of race, I am inexorably drawn back to it. I hope against hope that racism will die but it will not. I would like to write blue-sky, love poems, but they do not keep me awake at night wondering could I do more with the gifts God has given me. Racism is a volatile social force that creates an unseemly imbalance of power that is not offset by the appointment of a few dark faces to positions of privilege.

It is a mistake to accept the puerile notion that minority faces in high positions is the equivalent of progress. I would like to think that we have all matured beyond such a simplistic notion of life. I can think of at least three prominent examples at the level of federal government whose appointments have been shamefully fruitless. Figureheads are worthless.

In my deepest self, I am mindful of how well Americans – yea, people around the world – have become comfortable with the enigma of inequality. The beneficiaries of racism have grown so accustomed to their refined hatred and the prominence it gives them that they can't detect its poison in our culture. The victims of racism have grown either too tired to fight or too consumed with acceptance. Hence, they allow overt and covert offenses to go completely unchallenged. It has come to that.

Two recent incidents demonstrated both these societal truisms for me. First, I teach at a local university with a national reputation for training teachers. During class, I engaged my education students in a discussion about national and state education standards and introduced them to the concept of equity -- saying that despite standards, no two schools were the same. This spawned a frank discussion about whether every public school within a single district affords students the same chance to learn and be successful. What happened next shocked even me.

During the exchange, my Hispanic students began referring to "those bad children in the poor neighborhood." This was followed by a series of racially suggestive epithets. Upon further prompting, it became clear that they were referring to black students. I queried further only to hear more demeaning things like how "horrible and disrespectful those children were."

When I asked one student whether she realized the tone and context of her language demonstrated that she – as an aspiring teacher – was undervaluing *those* children (my veiled way of challenging her racism), she failed to recognize that saying these things could be construed as offensive. She only became more impassioned.

Even when another Hispanic classmate challenged her position, she never relented. She had revealed her feelings of superiority to the very children she might shortly be called upon to teach. She did not relent in saying that *those* children were worse than others.

She demonstrated one side of the problem. Racism is still a staple of daily life. She was a product of American acculturation – that unseen but very deliberate process by which we are inculcated into forming values about ourselves and others. Acculturation is where racism, the feeling that *others* are inferior, is born. Her beliefs were bred, not innate. They were the result of her formal and informal education.

The belief that black people are *other* people – a notion as common within Hispanic culture as any – is so endemic to American life that the problem of devaluing *other* people never troubles their spirits. If this were not so, there would be no "white Hispanics." Perhaps the thing most troubling about the aforementioned student-teacher interaction was that the student was only one semester away from a classroom that might contain *those* students.

The second event that reminded me of the ubiquitous quality of racism was an incident over breakfast. As I sat down to breakfast in a restaurant dreading the thought of a dentist's visit, I overheard a conversation between three young men seated at the next table – all around 17-19 years of age. One was black and the other two were white. I noticed them because they all looked as if they should have been in school at that hour.

During their conversation, the young, black man was called *nigger* at least three times in friendly fashion. What amazed me more than anything was that he showed no resentment, no challenge, no feeling of offense. Equally troubling was the fact that his counterparts felt an apparent ease in calling their *friend* nigger. They never flinched. Neither side took umbrage at the heinous tone of the conversation. Here was ignorance at breakfast.

Perhaps even more disturbing was the response I got from black parents to whom I recapitulated the story. They, too, seemed unfazed. They kept telling me, "oh, this is just the way young people speak to one another. They don't mean anything by it." I was shocked again. I could not see a Jewish child subjecting himself to ethnically or racially charged terms. I also do not believe his parents would tell me that negative names are harmless. That blacks have allowed the word *nigger* to become acceptable on any level is an ineffable failure.

We have failed to teach our children that this word nigger -- and its concomitant history -- are so offensive that it deserves no place in popular culture or modern language, not even as a term of endearment among friends. Some black people are so willing to be accepted that they are willing to countenance insults as affection. This is the embodiment – if I might borrow from Carter G. Woodson -- of the "mis-education of the negro."

Both groups – my students and the young men at breakfast -- were under twenty-five. I began to wonder if either group could know my discomfort with their indifference to racial prejudice. The discomfort was not for me, but for them. Children are not immune to hatred but are often ignorant of it or apathetic to it. I looked into their faces and saw why I cannot abandon this discussion of race.

Some things are wrong, and they are always wrong. Murder is wrong. Rape is wrong. Child abuse is wrong. There are no middle grounds for these crimes against humanity. One does not speculate or muse over the comparative quality of these crimes. They are always heinous – no exceptions. We know this because in almost every culture on earth these are crimes.

Likewise, racism is always wrong. There is no place for compromise. The difference with racism is that people are willing to engage in a sliding scale of moral justification. Americans engage too much in explaining away very real ethical problems via self-serving relativism. Cancer starts small and kills. Minute particles of poison render victims lifeless. A hint of racism taints a whole people.

Through the duplicity of mass media, America has reduced racism to a footnote in modern history. It is seen as a benign problem that existed for a time but was completely eradicated. Yet, racism lives. It is still deadly and impacts more people today than in years past. The difference is black people are less aware of it because the modes of aggression are subtle. *Today, racism stalks and kills with beautiful, quiet fury.*

Racism kills every day. Racism kills in inner cities. These squalid communities resemble the bombed out remains of war torn cities while stadiums and commercial projects go up nearby. The people are trapped and fight against drugs, gangs and gunfire. Racism kills with "all deliberate speed" in classrooms where black and minority students are suspended more often than anyone else, and tested into special education. Racism kills with professionalism in the workplace when blacks and minorities beat themselves bloody against glass ceilings. They all die by degrees.

The only remedy against ignorance is education. Money is not a remedy. It covers the fault, but does not cure it. Too many minority children measure success via the entertainer or the athlete. Entertainers – regardless of their seven figure incomes – are not immune to prejudice. Still, many young people are abandoning education for careers in entertainment. Youth incorrectly believe money is a fortress against injustice.

Recently, I listened to a former San Francisco 49er wide receiver during a televised interview on ESPN. He had been traded to the Baltimore Ravens but wanted to go to the

Philadelphia Eagles. As the interviewer challenged him about his choice, he kept reminding the player that he was the *property* of the Ravens. The term *property* was repeated several times. The interviewer seemed intent on reminding the player that he was *property*. It dawned on me that I had heard this term used about black men.

In 1857, the United States Supreme Court ruled that Dred Scott, a light-skinned black man, was not a United States citizen. The Court concluded that Dred Scott was *chattel*, a French word for *property*, not a citizen of the United States. Therefore, he could not sue to demand use of a train seat reserved for white citizens. The most deleterious notion in the case was that Dred Scott was declared *property*.

Yet, in the luxury of my gated community in 2004, I watched an athlete who is paid millions of dollars totally miss that he is considered *property* – valuable, but *property* nonetheless. I wondered if he knew about Dred Scott. It probably never crossed his mind that he and Dred Scott had the common problem of being seen as property despite the gap in time and income. Neither money nor privilege made the player any more valuable to Americans in 2004 than Dred Scott was to the United States Supreme Court in 1857.

Unlike Dred Scott, the player got his wish. He won the right to go to Philadelphia. He challenged the system and succeeded at choosing where he wanted to work. Yet, he was *property* in

San Francisco; he would have been *property* in Baltimore; and he will be *property* in Philadelphia.

Neither the player nor his interviewer could see the specter of Dred Scott permeating the television studio. However, he was there. Dred Scott could not sit on the train next to white people. The player can sit anywhere he pleases. He can buy any seat; however, he and Dred Scott will always be blood brothers.

Education is the single most powerful means of overcoming the limits of one's birth. For black Americans who are not born to privilege, education has consistently been a reliable means for turning tragedy into triumph. Blacks and Hispanics rely heavily upon public education as a conduit for children to be taught the basic skills needed to move either into the world of work or on to higher education.

However, the question presents itself: can the present public education system be trusted to properly educate all children? If the function of education is to prepare persons to enter society and become viable contributors, then education is the machine by which this has to be accomplished. Can minority parents rely upon public school systems to steer their children toward success?

The answer is no. The question is why? First, we still have a segregated and unequal school system that fails to provide all children with adequate educational resources. Second, more minority teachers are needed to counter the fact that nearly 40% of the student-aged population is minority. Third, and most important, there is an apparent unchecked strain of racism that affects the policies of school districts and allows minorities to be underprepared for the workforce. There is a move afoot in public education that puts minority children on the path toward failure rather than success. There is a clear presumption that they are not valuable. If actions are the measure of how much we care for black and minority children, then it is clear that they are unimportant.

Americans need to understand that we have not arrived at a place where race and discrimination do not matter. Racism has taken on a falsely benign character in America. Black and Hispanic Americans are sold an image of integration and success. Commercials with integrated casts, however, do not negate the reality that America's two largest minorities are still at the nadir of the social construct and that life for many minorities is below the general standard of living. How can the schools, the commercial life, the aesthetics of neighborhoods, and the sense of well-being be so drastically different in one part of town versus another?

The politicians have failed miserably at balancing these countervailing dichotomies. Since the 1970s we have had blacks at the helms of major cities. Washington, D.C., Chicago, Denver, Atlanta, Detroit, Cleveland and Birmingham, to name a few, all had black mayors; and you can still drive through either city and see the clear lines of demarcation between wealth and poverty. Black mayors are not the answer.

This brings me to another question: is the social construct of America defined more by class than race? The answer is no. Social theorists allege that classism has replaced racism. What they tend to miss, however, is that class is largely defined along racial lines. Class also does not have a 400 year legacy of tainting American history.

Gary Orfield of the Harvard Project points to a poignant demographic fact: eighty percent of white children do not go to school with minority children. When a school surpasses 40% in minority enrollment, whites move out. (Orfield, 2001) Residential housing patterns which determine the make up of schools also demonstrate that people choose to live separately.

Certainly they move out because they have the means, but, more importantly, they move out because they have the attitude that the school becomes less capable of educating their children because minority children are there. They move out because they believe that there is a downward turn in quality as neighborhoods change. "The average white person in metropolitan America lives in a neighborhood that is 80% white and 7% black." (Logan, 2001) Additionally, "[s]egregation patterns for whites from blacks, Hispanics and Asians persists today at about the same levels as was true in

1960." (Logan, 2001) Separate in America is a code word for "unequal." (Logan, 2002)

My concern is for those left behind. There must be a desire that these citizens are not consigned to live in a cauldron of poverty, poor education and limited career opportunities. We do understand that if left unaddressed, these problems will express themselves across the comfort of our gated lives via crime, illness and poverty.

My mission is to make America look in the mirror. How can we adopt a position of hegemony, telling Iraq and other countries how to treat their citizens when the richest country in the world exhibits the same class, racial and ethnic divisions as the countries it seeks to direct? If America's present position is so grand, how do we explain to the world why Randall Robinson would renounce America after spending his life fighting for blacks and other minorities? (Robinson, 2003)

If Randall Robinson could become an ex-patriot, what about the people in America's inner cities? I doubt the chances for those young people in the absence of a sound education and a strong family. This, again, is why education is important. These children must step on to a higher social tier. *If not, they will live in the parallel world from which you can see prosperity but never touch it.*

Randall Robinson and Shelby Steele, two premier scholars, hold at least two distinct positions on where blacks stand in America. Randall Robinson did not allow his personal success to divorce him from the proposition that others of his race were not as fortunate. Therefore, he devoted himself to issues of black equality and restitution (i.e., reparations) and to demanding that America live up to its Constitution. He believes that America has robbed blacks and owes them for the debt. (Robinson, 2000)

Steele published "The Age of White Guilt and the Disappearance of the Black Individual" in the November 2002 issue of *Harper's Magazine*. Steele prefers Americanized individualism. Steele's position is that black people maintain a sense of collective psyche in order to benefit from "white guilt" over past wrongs and to ". . . simply keep white folks on the hook." (Steele, 2002) Steele goes on to allege that black people are unable to move to a point of individual responsibility because they give more credence to white people's ability to oppress than to their own ability to transcend American racism through personal achievements. (Steele, 2002)

The contrast between Randall Robinson and Shelby Steele represents the present problem between the internal and external perception of where black Americans should be headed. Randall Robinson feels that America has not fulfilled its responsibility of righting past wrongs. He asserts that no matter what blacks do, America owes this debt and ought to pay it. Hence, whites should not be absolved of their obligation to acknowledge that their present success came at the expense of blacks.

Steele, conversely, believes that regardless of the past wrongs, black people should forget about whites and simply strive toward success. Steele goes on to assert that this requires a disconnect from black people in general. (Steele, 2002) He sees group responsibility as a burden. Hence, Steele says, "The greatest problem in coming from an oppressed group is the power the oppressor has over your group. The second greatest problem is the power your group has over you." (Steele, 2002)

My position is that for all their achievement, black and white Americans are inexorably linked by history. African-Americans can never move toward success in a country where they are now the second largest minority without collaboration. No matter how many blacks succeed individually, it is the success of the group that will affect life for the majority. Conversely, white Americans will never achieve the spiritual and historical liberation they desire nor will they achieve national greatness in the absence of an acknowledgement and payment of the debt they owe to African-Americans.

Black people are up against a growing tide of racism masked as class struggle. Fighting strategies must change in the struggle for basic equality because the American milieu has changed. For example, with the growth of the Hispanic population to 38.5 million citizens, blacks – only 38.3 million – are no longer the largest minority. Blacks are no longer the minority of choice.

America is in an age of wealth driven politics, a time when the influence of money controls social events. This latter statement is reinforced by the fact that the American Presidential race will cost the two candidates more than $200 million. Also, it is an election where two elites – both wealthy and graduates of Yale University – will square off in the election, claiming to understand the plight of the common man.

In his article "For Richer: How the Permissive Capitalism of the Boom Destroyed American Equality," Paul Krugman intimates that the Americans are relatively unaware of ". . . how much the gap between the very rich and the rest has widened over a very short period." (Krugman, 2002) The new standard of success is not to merely seek middle class status; rather, the dream now is to become a part of aristocracy. Krugman also points out that, "[t]he 13,000 richest families in America now have almost as much income as the 20 million poorest. And those families have incomes 300 times that of average [middle class] families." (Krugman, 2002)

He goes on to add that the continued concentration of wealth in the hands of a few is leading to ". . . more poverty and lower life expectancy." (Krugman, 2002) Our life expectancy is shorter than those of people in Canada, Japan and the larger nations of Western Europe. (Krugman, 2002) The goal of a middle class America has "unraveled" and turned into a societal strain between extreme poverty and extreme wealth. (Krugman, 2002) Also, there is a growing sense of indifference toward the less fortunate.

The key problem is that this growing wealthy class controls politics along with big business. Very few blacks find themselves among this elite group. Hence, we must consider the means by which the majority can make some progress out of their present class into the ranks of at least the middle class. Remember, the gap is growing between the wealthy and both the middle and poor classes. Additionally, the larger the wealthy class becomes, the more if will continue to influence politics and access to resources. It is this last problem that threatens blacks and minorities the most.

Krugman finally says, "As the gap between the rich and the rest of the population grows, economic policy increasingly caters to the interest of the elite, while public services for the population at large – above all, public education – are starved for resources." (Krugman, 2002) Krugman expresses the dire straits blacks and any other non-wealthy Americans will face – a desensitized elite that will have little pity on anyone else.

That being said, I want to explore the problems black Americans will face in such a society through the prism of public education. As with any critical issue in America, it may affect us all; but it will hurt black people worse. I believe that neither Robinson's dream of collective wholeness nor Steele's dream of individual independence can be realized without a larger class of black Americans who have entered the middle class and the aristocracy with the tools of the best and highest levels of education possible.

A good education is necessary to navigate in an increasingly complex world where understanding how to play the game means everything for survival. Education, not only the ability to acquire postsecondary degrees but the ability to decipher the code of societal issues, will mean the difference in an America that is inclusive versus one that is exclusive, provincial and desperate.

It is still education that will deliver most blacks from poverty, not entertainment or athletics. The number of celebrities in any racial or ethnic group is small. What is troubling is that some fifty years removed from *Brown v. The Board of Education of Topeka, Kansas* (1954), educational opportunities are being squandered by the majority of black and minority children via a number of misconceived notions. We must renew our commitment to education.

Chapter Two
The Importance of Education

Education must matter to black people. Black children who do not take advantage of education will become outcasts in this society. This very sobering fact cannot be ignored. In an age when technology and skills impact 85% of all jobs available, according to the United States Department of Labor, we cannot afford to be under prepared or unable to compete. Blacks must prepare themselves for the inevitability of a new social construct in which the world is no longer perceived in purely dichromatic terms.

Given the changing social milieu and the influx of immigrants who do not have the baggage of slavery and segregation in their American past, the game has changed. It has changed because America must take the needs of other groups into consideration. Blacks are no longer the prima donnas of American suffering.

Other people are here and are coming here in large numbers whose educational needs will be considered along with ours. They bring new issues of language and culture that deviate from the black-white conflicts of the past. Twenty-percent of school-age students speak a language other than English at home (Darden, 2003). The voices of immigrants resonate as clearly as our own. Also, they cannot be ignored.

Immigrants bring unlimited ambition, energy and a single-minded focus. Immigrants do care about American slavery or segregation. They believe in the nobility of the ideal America where anything is possible. This makes them more attractive to the American majority. They are more reminiscent of past generations of immigrants from Europe who came, labored and were incorporated into the American persona. Consequently, blacks will be supplanted by groups with a new social agenda, an agenda that cannot be couched solely in terms of conflicts between blacks and whites or the history those two groups have shared.

Hispanics have replaced blacks as America's largest minority. There are 38.5 million Hispanics and 38.3 million African-Americans. Yet, Hispanics are the most isolated ethnic group and they have the highest dropout rate in the country. (Nieto, 2003) Furthermore, there are more than one million black Hispanics in America. (Darden, 2003) Ironically, their plight isn't much different from that of African-Americans. According to the Lewis Mumford Center for Comparative Urban and Regional Research at the State University of New York, "[t]he socioeconomic profile of this group [i.e., black Hispanics] is more similar to that of non-Hispanic blacks than any other Hispanic groups." (Darden, 2003) And the "white Hispanics" tend to be affluent.

Hence, race matters even within ethnic groups. It should be noted, however, that the term Hispanic is an ethnic and not a racial designation. The terms "race" and "Hispanic" are fabrications. *Race and ethnicity are not the same. Race is color consciousness. Ethnicity is heritage, culture and language.* It is important that people know the difference. When discussions are had, these terms are often incorrectly used interchangeably. Each has its own history and connects a different philosophical perspective.

For my part, even though the discussion here will be couched in terms of the needs of black children. I want the same things for all children of all races and ethnicities. Poor white children are not served by the American education system any better than minority children. Native-American children's educational problems mirror those of black and Hispanic children in our inner cities. Good education is needed for all children. All poor children get shortchanged in public schools.

I would also like to add that the fight for fair public education is not for the mere benefit of minorities. America will never realize its vision for itself without fair treatment of its minority populations. While Asians are deemed the "model minority," blacks and Hispanics are struggling to achieve academically. They represent more than 70 million Americans whose fates are tied to the fate of the country's education system. Hence, all Americans have a vested interest in their success.

Gated communities will not keep out the ills that will be loosed within these borders if these groups are marginalized into poverty and desperation.

The poor see education as the one means by which they can rise above their humble beginnings. According to Kathleen Vail, "[t]o many children, urban schools are their best, last hope." (Vail, 2003) We need a system worthy of that confidence. Education is the cheapest and most reliable means by which impoverished people can make the move up the social ladder. At the very least, it increases their chances dramatically. The earning potential of a person with a bachelors degree is double that of a person with a high school diploma. (Nieto, 2003)

Education is important. The United States Supreme Court knew this when it issued its decision in *Brown v. Board of Education of Topeka, Kansas* (1954), some fifty years ago. The Court said:

> Today, education is perhaps the most important function of state and local governments. . . Today, it is the principal instrument in awakening the child to cultural values, to preparing him for later professional training, and in helping him to adjust normally to his environment. In these days, it is doubtful that any child may reasonably be expected to succeed in life if he is denied the opportunity of an education.

Opportunity for a quality education is the crux of the matter. Our children's future depends upon their ability to gain access to public education that is fair. To date, neither local nor state governments have met the test of equal education for all children. That goal remains elusive.

It is this business of being denied the opportunity that troubles me. Children in schools with minority populations are not being given the same chance. There is no similarity between the two worlds of minority children in poor neighborhoods and that of white students in wealthy areas. Neither group of children is responsible for where they are born or to whom they are born. But government's job is to use its vast resources to balance the disparity for the public good.

Although its judgment was bifurcated in the recent University of Michigan case where the issue was the potential discriminatory effect of Affirmative Action, the Supreme Court reaffirmed that access to a good education is still life determinative. (Darden, 2003) Therefore, if the highest Court in the land has held that education is vital for more than fifty years, state and local governments should act with some sense of earnestness and urgency about the education of minority children.

The sad truth is that neither local nor state government has answered the challenge. Black and minority children are receiving nothing close to an equal education compared to their white counterparts. I believe this is more by design than happenstance; however, the result in either instance is an inferior educational experience for minority children which opens the door for greater levels of poverty and dependence. In addition, it creates for America that needed underclass that will work for low wages. Capitalism requires poor people and cheap labor. Someone has to be on the bottom.

There are a number of factors that impact the quality of education for black and minority children. First, it is a travesty that the students with the greatest needs get the worst teachers. For example, African-American students often receive teachers who have lower expectations for them than for their white students. (Hrabowski, 2003) In schools with high rates of poverty and high minority student populations, ". . . approximately 30% of core courses [i.e., mathematics, language arts, science and social studies] are taught by teachers who lack certification in those courses." (Haycock, 2003)

These same schools are also burdened with an overabundance of teachers who are inexperienced, lacking in subject matter expertise and ineffective. (Haycock, 2003) How can low performing students with low performing teachers produce anything but poor academic results and low test scores? It does not take a rocket scientist to conclude that if the children who need the most help are getting the worst teachers they will perform poorly academically and on standardized tests.

This is critical when research demonstrates that a sequence of good or bad teachers influences academic and life outcomes. Teacher quality "can represent the difference between entry into a selective college and a lifetime of working at McDonalds." (Haycock, 2003) Moreover, the best teachers prefer not to work in schools with high minority populations. (Orfield, Frankenburg, Lee, 2002) Black students are up to two times more likely than white students to be assigned the most ineffective teachers. (Haycock, 2003) Again, comparisons between white students and minority students make no sense when the two groups are not being given similar resources in their preparation.

If two world-class athletes are put on the same track in the Olympic Games, and one has been given a steady diet of bad foods while the other has followed a strict diet of high protein, their performances will differ dramatically. There will be an *achievement gap*. The longer the two are exposed to antithetical modes of preparation, the greater the likelihood that the competition will eventually become no contest. Similarly, when black and minority children are given a steady diet of bad teachers and are asked to compete with white students who have had better, more experienced and certified teachers, how can their be anything but an achievement gap?

The injustice is that the minority students are blamed. The poor achievement that follows this pattern of policy and administrative neglect is laid at the feet of children. How so? Well, when state assessments are administered and children are prevented from being promoted from grade to grade or are prevented from graduating from high school or are unprepared for college entrance examinations, where does the fault lie but in an educational system that bred them for failure? Yet, the children bear the consequences.

Furthermore, this pattern of the most high-risk students being saddled with the least effective teachers speaks volumes about whether we value poor and minority children. (Nieto, 2003) Teachers in most cases serve at the discretion of their superintendent. They can be assigned where they are needed. Unless there is some union rule to the contrary, teachers can be placed anywhere in the district. I wonder why decision makers cannot bring themselves to mandate that better teachers be placed in schools with minority populations. Also, the best principals belong in the neediest schools. Is the failure to act a choice of omission or an act of racism?

Second, there is the ever present issue of race. America continues to try to sell the public on the issue that race does not matter. However, it is a truism that whites do not want their children to attend schools with minority children – especially black children. One Erie County, New York official put it bluntly. He said he moved his children out of Buffalo public schools and into a "suburban" [a euphemism for white, wealthy] school because "his youngsters were becoming afraid of black kids." (Darden, 2003) If a public official would be so crass, it is no surprise that when minority student populations increase, whites still take flight. Implicit in the statement of the Erie County official mentioned above, is racism, not concerned parenting.

This "forget-the-rest" attitude is commonplace. One ". . . *New Republic* columnist readily agreed that the honors program in his daughter's school in Montgomery County, Maryland amounted to a 'school-within-a-school' for white and Asian students – and then announced that if this program were eliminated, he would pull his daughter out of that school in a nanosecond . . . ." (Quoted in Kohn, 1998) Kohn also quotes Amy Stuart Wells as saying, "We like the fact that our kids are in desegregated schools but that the fact that the white children are in the top classes and blacks are in the bottom is someone else's problem." (Kohn, 1998)

This kind of provincialism of the well-off has become standard fare. Whites want what's best for their children; the corollary is all other children be damned. (Kohn, 1998) According to Dale Maharidge, this group ". . . sends its children to private schools, sometimes employs private police, and lives behind literal or symbolic walls."

(Maharidge, 1993) Again, these attitudes represent an insidious trend toward openly racist leanings. Racism has become politically correct.

Miami-Dade County, Florida is the consummate example of this trend. As the Hispanic population increased from the 1950s through the 1980s, the presence of whites in the city and white students in the public schools fell dramatically. Whites moved to West Broward County and Palm Beach County. Today, the student population in Miami is minority-majority with Hispanics and blacks representing the two largest groups. Miami has the fourth largest school district in the nation with an annual budget of 4.3 billion dollars. It has a student population that is 60% Hispanic and 34% black. This is odd in a city that was predominantly white just forty years ago. Where did they go and why?

Perhaps the answer is as simple as no wants to speak about race. Edwin Darden says, "[Race] is a taboo, acknowledged but rarely discussed in public." (Darden, 2003) People react to it almost constantly, but they absolutely do no want to talk about its impact on education. For example, how often does one hear that the achievement gap between whites and children of color has grown in recent years? (Nieto, 2003) Martin Habersham, a University of Wisconsin professor, exposes the heart of the problem. He says, "Race, persists as a barrier in public education because it accomplishes the mission of providing one class of people with access and privilege; and at the same time, it maintains an infrastructure of failure for another group." (Habersham quoted in Darden, 2003)

These pathways toward success and failure are at the heart of public education. People do not want to acknowledge that racism is an important tool in continuing the stratification of our society into levels of poverty and wealth. Yet, in understanding the problems of the modern education system, ". . . talking about race is something people are unwilling to do." Race is a barrier to school reform. (Darden, 2003)

As a result, a problem like the resegregation of public schools goes almost unnoticed. Schools are as segregated today as they were in 1970. (Orfield, Frankenberg, Lee, 2003) Schools have become quietly resegregated and no one so much as raises the issue. Moreover, that fact that we cannot have rational dialogue on the subject is a disgrace. (Darden, 2003) The issue of resegregation is problematic because minority schools are allowed to persist in poverty, low academic performance, violence, and a general malaise of hopelessness.

School boards are at a loss for how to fix these problems whether or not they have the will to do it. The Chicago school system, for example, spent more than $20 billion dollars over twenty years to address segregation and reached no solution. (Vail, 2003) It is no wonder that Judge Charles P. Kocoras, looking at the futility and waste of trying to implement the desegregation consent decree declared the Chicago model a failure and deemed the decree itself "passé." (Korocas quoted in Vail, 2003)

The untold legacy of these failed efforts to desegregate schools is that they were never meant to succeed, and ill-guided efforts to desegregate schools left wounds of racism in places like Boston and New York that are so deep that those cities remain on the verge of massive racial conflict at the slightest spark. (Vail, 2003) Boston's urban schools are 25% white while their suburban schools are 80% white. (Vail, 2003)

Despite an increasingly multicultural consciousness outside school, students are exposed less and less to people of other races and ethnicities in the classroom. This means that they may not engage in daily interaction with blacks or Hispanics or other minorities until they reach college or the workplace. This delayed contact gives time for stereotypes and prejudices to take root.

I attended all black schools throughout my years in public school, an all black undergraduate school and an all black university before encountering white students in 1988 at the University of Miami School of Law. I was twenty-four before I ever sat next to a white person in a classroom. I discovered from the tone of our discussions that many of my counterparts had lived similarly isolated experiences.

Up to that point, whites were nonessential to my life; and for them blacks had been, at best, on the periphery of their existence. So, there was a blatant insensitivity to our presence. They spoke candidly about race as if we were not there. I spoke candidly about race because it has always mattered in my world. What became obvious was not so much that they hated black people; but they knew nothing more of us than stereotypes. They did not think we were relevant because they had grown up in a world where blacks were of no consequence.

I will never forget how callously they spoke of overturning the *Brown v. Board of Education (1954)* decision during my Constitutional Law class. They talked about the case as a legal aberration, not based on law. I, knowing that *Brown* had been my key to accessing law school, argued for my sacred passport. They said *Brown* should be overturned. I discovered that we saw the world through different eyes.

I became aware that our mutual isolation had caused us to harbor prejudices. The difference was that they were a part of white society and could afford to think me irrelevant. I was from Overtown and Liberty City, two of Miami's oldest and poorest black enclaves. It is not possible for a black person to live in peace and ignore the potential threat of white power. I had lived through race riots in 1968, 1980 and 1982. I persist in looking at the problem today because the conditions that spawned those outbursts have gone unaddressed. Education was not the least among these.

When it comes to public education, for example, power is exerted daily to the detriment of black and minority children. There is a political price to pay when whites stand up against racism. (Darden, 2003) This is why most whites will not openly contest racism. Hence, ". . . 43% of the nation's minority children remain isolated in separate—and decidedly unequal – urban schools." (Darden, 2003)

High levels of poverty persist in minority schools. As much as people try to separate the two, poverty and high minority populations tend to go hand in hand. Poverty and race are inextricably tied together when it comes to trying to solve the problems of unequal education opportunities for minority children. (Orfield, Frankenberg, Lee, 2003) The two cannot be separated. Scholars such as Richard Kahlenberg have suggested new educational models based on developing middle class environments through an admixture of wealthy, middle class and poor students. He believes that simply being around students of a higher economic genre will increase academic performance for poor students. (Kahlenberg, 2001)

What Kahlenberg's hypothesis overlooks is that these neighborhoods are impoverished because their tax bases are undermined. School funding is primarily contingent upon local real property taxes. When that tax base erodes, schools are less able to provide similar resources to all schools. Supreme Court cases throughout the 1970s and 1980s argued the issue of equity as concerning neighboring cities that refused to share funding with poorer school districts. At least one city in Vermont is prepared to secede from its home state and join New Hampshire to prevent mandated sharing of school funding costs.

Kahlenberg's position is also weakened by the fact that laws have not been able to prevent folk from moving whenever a school reached minority-majority status. Remember, the mantra of the Erie County official mentioned earlier in this discussion. People have their preferences. And sometimes that means that they simply refuse to allow their children to interact with minority children. White students attend schools that are more than 80% white. (Orfield, Frankenberg, Lee, 2003) This is not just because they can afford to live in exclusive neighborhoods; it is also because they choose to separate themselves from minorities.

Still, for the present, poverty creates an overwhelming problem in public schools. Twenty-six million children are participating in the Title I funded program which has given additional monies to schools since its advent in 1965. For thirty-nine years, money has been used as a panacea for poverty. Yet, poverty persists and low performing schools persist. We know that children who begin their lives in poverty come to school with a host of concerns that may never be overcome. For example:

> Children from high poverty environments enter school less ready to learn and lag behind their more affluent classmates in ability to use language. They face higher rates of health problems . . . They are more likely to drop out of school, get pregnant at an early age or have a hard time paying attention because they don't eat breakfast and may not have had dinner the night before. (Vail, 2003)

Poverty places children at a disadvantage at the starting line. Here is another fact that replicates itself in schools with high minority populations. Poverty, combined with problems of race and ethnicity, may be at the heart of why only 60% of Hispanics and 73% of African-Americans graduate compared to 88% of white students. (Hrabowski, 2003)

Poverty also provides a breeding ground for poor self-concept. African-American and Hispanic children tend to have a low estimate of their own ability to perform academically compared to white students. (Hrabowski, 2003) When this is coupled with teachers who also have lower expectations for these same students, we are assured a result of low academic achievement in the end. (Hrabowski, 2003)

We have an education system that robs black and minority children of their chances for success very early on. Black and Hispanic children are assigned to special education more often than any other children, and at the same time, they are grossly underrepresented in gifted classes. (Darden, 2003) Additionally, the average 12th grade student of color reads at a level equal to that of an average white student in the 8th grade. (Nieto, 2003) Of course, dropout rates and poor rates of graduation further demonstrate the disparity in the educational experience each student is receiving.

The dramatic end result is that minority children are receiving an inferior education which prepares them for nothing except to lose out in the competition for jobs that pay the kind of wages that make the American dream possible. Why is there no outcry from all quarters rather than just from blacks or minorities? Is this the kind of society we want?

Now, the hard question must be asked. How can these things be? How can a society that is so rich in resources have failed to undo the _Plessy v. Ferguson_ (1896) world of separate and unequal education and separate and unequal life experiences? However, the real answer is that America needs minorities to fail. Quality teachers and schools have an impact on students that not only provides them with a sound education but also provides them access to the pathways to privilege and power that make life easier. (Nieto, 2003) Our presently bifurcated school system denies minority students access to opportunity.

Education remains an important resource. It is vital to the uplift of individuals and to social groups. Every immigrant group that has come to American since its inception has used education as a means for building wealth, improving social standing, establishing political presence and providing an improved outlook for future generations. They have used education to move from poverty to the middle class or higher.

However, black and minority children today are faced with a system that has no intention of integrating the majority of them into American culture. The system I described here can do little more than increase levels of frustration and reinforce poor self-concept, making black and minority children ripe for prison – one of our fastest growing industries. America is not above creating a plan for its dispensable citizens.

Given that blacks and Hispanics rank first and second in America's prison population, one can readily see the end result of poor education. Blacks are 12% of the national population and nearly 50% of the prison population. (Harrison and Beck, 2001) What is even more startling is the apparent connection between poor educational levels and rates of incarceration. Sixty-eight percent of state prisoners did not earn a high school diploma. (U.S. Department of Justice, 2004) The American education system is doing a disservice to its minority populations at a time when a good education means everything.

There must be a radical change in the public education model in order to serve the needs of children who come to school needing so much. Many school districts are trying everything from reducing mobility rates to in-school clinics to shore up these children as they try to prepare them for learning. But the problem still remains that race plays a role in educational decision making. And whether or not blacks hold positions of power, there continues to be example after example of blatant disregard for the lives of minority children.

Here's just one example. Miami Edison Senior High School earned its fourth grade of "F" at the end of the 2003-04 school year. Edison earned two "D's" and four "F's" in a six year period. (www.dadeschools.net) Its population is predominantly Haitian-American. The principal retired after earning a third "F." Subsequently, the district leadership demonstrated questionable decision-making by appointing a minimally qualified principal at the beginning of 2003-04. After little more than two months, the students staged a walkout and the principal was reassigned. He was replaced by a retired principal. He retired again. Hence, the school with the worst annual state evaluations in the county had four principals in a one year period.

The simple truth is the school deserved the best principal available. When you have a crisis in a large organization, you should send your best troubleshooter, not someone who learns on the job.

Why didn't this Miami Edison get the best principal? Can a school system claim to value students when its actions demonstrate the contrary? This is no sleight against the young principal.

I could be wrong, but anyone with a modicum of intelligence knows that when you have a problem in a $4.3 billion dollar organization, you put your best qualified person on the job. Low performing schools are at a point of crisis. Who sends an underprepared administrator to handle a crisis except a school board in a public education setting? What did the decision to assign an inexperienced principal to Miami Edison Senior High School say about whether those children were valued? It showed that those children and parents were regarded as unimportant. It showed intent for these black children to fail.

Here again, you have an example of students who need the best getting inexperienced leadership. Did anyone expect this to work? Miami Edison suffers from the same issues that thwart success in other schools with high minority populations such as low expectations for students, poor teacher quality, segregation, and poverty. It is a Title I school. How then could this school possibly be expected to overcome its previous track record of three Fs with this kind of administrative disruption?

The critical question is: does anyone in power care about these children? Haitians have the burden of black skin in a country where being black makes you unimportant. So, it is no surprise that they have not been given the best chance to succeed. Their treatment is totally in keeping with the patterns we have discussed throughout this chapter. It is also in keeping with the discriminatory behavior shown toward Haitians in the community by INS, the courts, and local governmental officials. This occurred at Miami Edison Senior High School in spite of the very well-documented truism that segregated schools produce lower levels of achievement. (Orfield, Frankenberg, Lee, 2003) I might add here that all four high schools that earned an "F" in Miami on the 2002-03 assessment were predominantly black, had black principals and were located in the inner city.

The American education system is in a state of disaster as it concerns minority children. White children and minority children receive vastly different educational experiences and the results for each group are just as polarized. The fact that we live in an ever-growing multicultural society does not change the fact that minorities are being cheated.

We cannot be afraid to acknowledge that racism is present in public education. Nor can we hesitate to point out that race makes the majority of Americans indifferent to this fact. Education matters. Race matters. The consequences of being poorly prepared for life after school also matters. If we continue to be silent, we will doom yet another generation of children to inferior educations in a world where globalization means that the best educated prevail.

Education is about more than information. It is also about one's ability to participate in life. American society judges you on your pedigree. The best means by which pedigree can be changed or social standing improved is education. However, if students who enter the educational system with disadvantages are further crippled by a system that teaches them nothing, saddles them with inferior teachers, gives them inexperienced administrators and fails them for not achieving, they cannot win.

Someone must take up this challenge of seeing that all children receive an equal educational experience. Equity, the simple ability for a minority student to receive the same quality of education as the white student, is presently unavailable. Minority children are not inferior students. The failures of their schools and the school systems that breed failing schools are not their fault.

Chapter Three
Equal at the Start

What is the achievement gap? The term is misleading because it suggests that minority children are not achieving or are incapable of achieving at the same levels as their white counterparts. The term wrongly places the onus for failure upon the shoulders of children. The term achievement gap is fraught with problems. There is a gap, but it is one of preparation that leads to a gap in performance; furthermore, the gap is not engendered by biological, intellectual nor genetic defects.

A few years ago, I sat on a committee whose focus was the achievement gap in my school district. The group was comprised of some of the best minds in the school district, community and business leaders, NAACP representatives, and university professors. I sat there intrigued by the subject and listened intently to the exchanges. Yet, never did anyone ever question the validity of the gap from the perspective that all children begin school relatively close in ability but begin to diverge in performance as early as second or third grade.

No one questioned that the gap was not an inherent intellectual flaw in children but an inbred practice of failure brought on by a sorting process that put some children on the path toward success and others on a path toward poverty. As I saw it, the gap -- that difference in academic performance and in performance on state assessments -- was engendered by systemic miseducation, not a function of the inabilities or disabilities of children. The gap was another way of converting racism into intellectual propaganda; it smacked too much of racism masquerading as scholarly analysis.

Moreover, when I heard any discussion of the "gap," it never included data on poor white students. Poor whites who receive inferior education are equally affected by levels of poverty. They are also inclined to perform poorly in academic settings. Yet, much of the conversation surrounding the gap among educators tends to focus on blacks and Hispanics. Whites in poverty are seldom discussed. Poverty, however, has the same effect in Africa, Latin America, the United States, Miami, Detroit or Philadelphia.

To verify my suspicion, I reviewed the work of a colleague. Dr. Linda Sorhaindo, a researcher and statistical analyst for Miami-Dade County Public Schools, concluded her engaging doctoral dissertation by looking at poverty and student performance in a unique way. Her central thesis was that levels of poverty negatively impact student achievement. (Sorhaindo, 2003) This was a unique approach because most scholars acknowledge that poverty, as a general concept, hinders student performance; but Linda postulated and proved that the deeper and more persistent the poverty, the more the child is impacted in the classroom.

(Sorhaindo, 2003) "Lawrence Aber, former director of the *National Center for Children in Poverty* in New York City, says the deeper the poverty, the more powerful its impact on a child's life." (Quoted in Vail, 2003)

Poverty yields the same results in all children, regardless of race. Poverty's concomitant evils -- poor health, high family mobility, poor self-esteem, inability to concentrate -- can render any child of any race or ethnicity less effective. Hence, when educators talk about the achievement gap as it pertains to race or ethnicity and leave out white children impacted by poverty, there is reason for disbelief about the conclusions and for room to question those making the conclusions. We also know that student performance can be impacted negatively as much as 30 points for every $10,000 difference in household income. (Darden, 2003) So, when race rather than poverty is used as the measuring stick for learning potential, there is a chance that racism is standing in the "gap."

Perhaps the trouble in the traditional analysis of associating low performance with race or ethnicity is understandable to a degree. When one looks at society, for the most part, levels of wealth are also fairly divisible along lines of race and ethnicity. Blacks and Hispanics are disproportionately represented among the poor. For example, in 2003 the number of black Americans in poverty increased from "22.7% to 24.1% in one year." (Darden, 2003) Also, as many as 200,000

Hispanic children fell into poverty according to statistics for the year 2000. (Darden, 2003) Scholars are beginning to look at socioeconomic status rather than race or ethnicity as ". . . the best indicator of academic success." (Darden, 2003) My point here is that race is not the cause of the disparities in scores between whites and minorities. Rather, it is why children are treated differently in school systems. One group receives better preparation and better resources to learn than the others.

Educators have the penchant for adopting terminology that carries with it a plethora of ills about children. Much of that terminology tends to label children as failures. This notion of an achievement gap is one such intellectual abyss into which educators have fallen; they are completely unaware of the sins this phrase engenders when it is applied to minority children.

The term "achievement gap" tends to lay the cause for the poor test results on the children rather than on the system that produces these results. *I have yet to see a school system designed and administered by children. It is the adults, not the children who are failing.* The adults err, and the children bear the consequences.

The gap is itself a fallacy. The gap should not apply to the children; rather, it should apply to the adults who promulgate policies within our school systems that place black and minority children at the mercy of ill-prepared teachers in dilapidated buildings. The gap is separate and unequal education experiences. From the time they enter public school systems until the time they leave, minority children are subjected, more often than their white peers, to inferior resources. Then, they are asked to measure up to white children who have lived in a parallel world of plenty. That is an act of racism.

In truth, genetic research, biological anthropology and religion remind us that we all have a common beginning. We all are equal at the start. So, from whence cometh the gap, the point at which black and minority children diverge into this pattern of failures and shortcomings? At the very core of this problem of devaluing minority children is the issue of the kind of society we want.

Building a nation in which some 70 million minority people in America are exposed to the lowest quality of education cannot be good for the whole nation. We are taking people who start out as equals and grooming some for failure. That is what the education system described in the previous chapter is designed to do. If it were not designed to do this, then educators would prevent the continued destruction of young minds.

This is not victimhood. All too often, we want to diffuse the fact that racism exists and is activated through administrative policies by saying that blacks or minorities operate from a disposition of powerlessness based on being victimized by society. (Steele, 2001) While I admit there is some misguided thinking, that does not negate the fact that American society will victimize anyone or any group for the benefit of the white power structure. We saw this in the 1988 election when Willie Horton's black visage (Horton killed someone while out on a weekend furlough) was used to propel George H. W. Bush pass Michael Dukakis. (Swain, 2002) We saw this again in California in 1993 when Governor Pete Wilson sought to victimize Mexicans by calling for tougher immigration laws in order to win votes. (Maharidge, 1993) We saw it yet again in 2004 when Governor Gray Davis sought to win Hispanic voters in his attempt to thwart his recall prior to his subsequent loss to Arnold Schwarzenegger. In a desperate attempt to win votes, Davis called for relaxing measures to obtain legal identification such as a driver's license.

The offended parties here were not minorities retreating into victimhood. They were minorities victimized by whites who would do anything to win political power. It happens in every Presidential election. Promises are made and not kept. Hence, the argument that a sense of victimhood controls our destiny is only partially true, if at all. Racism is real and potent. It is the trump card played in every national election. If one truly understands its breath, there is reason to develop a sense of being victimized. I am not saying that victimhood should control anyone, but neither can it be dismissed as unimportant.

Children are too precious to leave to the devices of prejudice. They are too precious to leave to happenstance. Our dealings with them and on their behalf must be nobler. My goal is to eradicate the residue of racist thinking that allows many educators to start out feeling that the black children, in particular, are presumably ignorant.

Teachers have lower expectations for black and Hispanic students. (Hrabowski, 2003; Rolon, 2003) Teachers who begin with this presumption are not inclined to do their best. If the teacher believes that the student cannot learn, then that child is doomed. In order to address the assumed ignorance of minority children, allow me to digress here into the matter of our collective inheritance.

I suggest we begin at the beginning. Dr. Spencer Wells, a noted geneticist, published *The Journey of Man: A Genetic Odyssey* in 2002. In his book, Dr. Wells traces the genetic history of all human beings. His work is an update to that of the 1987 group led by Rebecca Cann, Michael Stoneking, and Allen Wilson. In 1987, they conducted a study of the mitochondrial DNA of women from around the world and concluded that all human beings could trace their genetic ancestry back to an African woman called "Eve." (Kottak, 1991) Their research put modern man in sub-Saharan Africa approximately 200,000 years ago. This reinforced the notion that everyone started in the same place.

In 2003, G. Phillip Rightmire, a New York State University paleontologist, discovered three 160,000 year old skulls in Ethiopia. He surmised that ". . . the skulls provide the clearest evidence to date for an African origin of modern humans, and strikes another blow against the idea that humans had a multi-regional origin both within and outside Africa." (Rightmire, 2003) The crux of Rightmire's conclusion was that all people descended from a common African ancestry.

So, when Dr. Wells, using the advantages of the demystified human genome, applied his ample intellect to tracing the historical movement of early man, is there any wonder that he finds man standing in the savannahs of Africa about 60,000 years ago. (Wells, 2002) Wells goes on to literally track the movement of modern man from Africa (60,000 years ago) to Southern Asia to Australia (50,000 years ago) to the Middle East (45,000 years ago) to Eastern Asia (40,000 years ago) and to Europe (30,000 years ago).

Wells does this through the identification of genetic markers or variants that occur less frequently in peoples the shorter their time out of Africa. (Wells, 2002) Wells found that the highest rate of variation occurs in Africans, making them the world's oldest people. (Wells, 2002) Hence, genetic research has confirmed our common African origin. I repeat; we are all Africans.

The beauty of Wells' research is that he was able to map the progress of modern man along geographic routes based upon his study of man's genetic evolution. It is this combination of geography and genetics that makes Wells' research special. Wells points out that Europeans were the last to emerge in the chain of genetic evolution and last in terms of modern man's departure out of Africa. Wells notes that the first Africans that yielded modern man were probably dark skinned. (Wells, 2002) He postulates that the first group to leave eastern African went to Australia. Is it not strange then that the modern black people whose skin most resembles Wells' African "Adam" are today the brunt of a racist philosophy that makes them last?

Although the dates in these three significant finds by Cann, Rightmire and Wells may differ as to the exact age of modern man, one undeniable fact is that East Africa is the collective birthplace of modern humans. Another salient point not to be overlooked is that we all have the same genetic makeup and the same starting point. It does not seem far-fetched to conclude that at birth we all start out equal or at least relatively so. I should add that Wells finds the notion of races antiquated, if not ridiculous.

Let me add also the Biblical perspective. In Genesis 2:7, the Bible says "And the Lord God formed man out of the dust of the ground and breathed into his nostrils the breath of life, and man became a living soul."(Bible, KJV) I particularly like this passage for the intimacy it shows in God's connection with man. Breath or wind in the Bible is always associated with life force. One can almost see in this passage the first act of CPR. This is the Christian story of man's origin. However, whether you believe the Bible or the Torah or the Koran, the result is still the same. All mankind is believed to have a common origin. Again, we are all the same at the start.

Then, there is the whole field of brain research. Educators are beginning to look seriously at how the brain's development contributes to learning. But even here, the proof leads to a similar conclusion. Brain research shows that we are generally born with approximately 100 billion brain cells. Again, the same brain is found at birth in all races and ethnicities. Divergence begins to occur in the early period of development between 0-3 years of age.

Stimulation, or the lack thereof, affects the growth of the synaptic pathways that allow the brain to learn. Studies have demonstrated that a child who receives ample stimulation is prone to be a better learner over time than one who does not. Still, this is an after the fact problem. But in the beginning, the brains are generally the same.

So, if genetic research, anthropology, religious thinking and brain research all confirm a single origin for mankind, minority students should not be presumed ignorant. Educators should arrive at the conclusion that all children can be taught. The problem is this: are we willing to commit the same resources or additional resources when they are needed to afford children an equal chance? We do know that children entering school out of poverty need more assistance. "They are behind before their academic career has a chance to start." (Vail, 2003)

However, it should be noted that the academic disadvantage noted here is not biologically but sociologically generated by a lack of pre-school preparation. (Vail, 2003) For example, if a new student is plagued by the problems of high mobility due to poverty, that can affect the child's readiness to learn. Some school districts struggle with mobility rates as high as 70%. (Vail, 2003) "Students who move frequently feel apart from the school community and are less engaged." (Vail, 2003) This is not a lack of intelligence; it is a lack of time to focus on learning.

When high mobility is coupled with teacher apathy, low expectations or poor teacher quality, there is bound to be a negative result. These are not problems of race or ethnicity but problems of a social nature. The difficulty here is getting educators to see the difference and to root out the presumption that certain students cannot learn. They can learn, but it will simply take more to make it happen. This cannot be done in an atmosphere where there is a belief that some children are superior to others.

This is the core of the problem. How did we arrive at the conclusion that some cultures are superior to others? How have we arrived at the notion that some people are superior to others? The truth is Americans refuse to release themselves from old notions of racial and ethic superiority. In spite of all the talk to the contrary, we are Balkanizing into ethnic, social and racial groups with the intent of living provincial lives, judging our counterparts as inferior from afar.

Dale Maharidge says that we are retreating to three distinct groups. He says:

> American separatists come in three major forms. The first are the products of what [former] Labor Secretary Robert Reich terms the "succession of the successful." This de facto oligarchy sends its children to private schools, sometimes employs private police, and lives behind literal or symbolic walls. . . The second kind of separatist is quite involuntary. . . They are millions of working, service-sector poor, the jobless factor hands, the homeless. . . The third kind of separatist withdraws culturally. While immigrants have historically rushed to assimilate, their modern counterparts often live in isolation. (Maharidge, 1993)

This factionalizing of America defies the notion of a melting pot (Maharidge, 1993). Even worse, the public school systems of the country are being used to perpetuate and strengthen this American devolution. When the bulk of what our schools produce in terms of students is unusable, what can we do but assume that the schools need an overhaul?

Moreover, population separation is generating an atmosphere where children are viewed through refracting lenses of prejudice. Teachers are citizens of our society. They are not immune from bringing their misgivings to class with them. Lisa Delpit, in her book *Other People's Children: Cultural Conflict in the Classroom (1995)*, has postulated that it is not the children's inability to learn but the teacher's inability to connect with those learners that causes the students to disconnect from the learning process. Delpit uses cogent examples from her work with African-Americans, Native-American, and Polynesian children to demonstrate the need for teachers to know and value their students' culture in order to effectively implement pedagogical practices. (Delpit, 1995)

In order to work with all children, teachers must believe in all of them. The children who come to school from poor homes are just playing catch up. The question is: will we give each of them the same opportunity to learn? Teachers have no control over the students they get, but they do have control over the environment that the children enter and the treatment that the children get in those classrooms. Teachers have the ability to learn about the neighborhoods where they work. I recommend to my pre-service teachers that they at least drive through the neighborhoods where they will be assigned.

Still, we cannot ignore the fact that something is happening to minority children within the walls of our schools. When the rate of graduation for white students is over 80% and it is only 56% for Hispanic students, something is wrong. (Nieto, 2003) "Given these alarming statistics, the claim that education is equally available to all is more of a fiction than ever." (Nieto, 2003)

Just from my own observation, we receive eager students for the most part at kindergarten. However, by the time they reach the end of elementary school, students have already begun to lose their love for education. We must begin to look at the breaking points and determine what is occurring. There is no room for fault-finding. It is my hope that real collaboration will take place, that racism will be acknowledged and that poverty will be addressed.

One thing I am certain of, however, is that the children are not defective. They need different levels of intervention. They need people who believe they are worth the investment of their professional energy. They need support. We do not have an alternative to helping children succeed. Our workforce depends upon it. Our societal structure depends upon it. Our financial stability depends upon it.

I challenge America here to recognize that race matters. I further challenge America to invest as heavily in children and schools as we have in guns. We need to declare a war on poor education. I certainly hope that effort does not degenerate into the kind of dysfunctional program we used to address our war on drugs. The field of education is full of great minds. I do hope that each professional will commit himself to teaching even more assiduously.

One final thing to consider is the end game. If black and minority students are not performing well, it means that fewer and fewer of them are making it into college. It was a common truism throughout the 1990's that there were more black males in prison than college – 800,000 in prison, 600,000 in college. Well, when you look at the number of blacks becoming professionals, there is a continuous downturn.

For example, there is a growing crisis in the field of medicine. Blacks represented only 4.5% of physicians in America in 2001. (ETS, 2004) Also, ETS reports that ". . . the educational pipeline becomes increasingly more constricted as it passes through each milestone in the youth development period, and the flow into 'well-prepared' pool is more constricted for [black] males than for females." (ETS, 2004) In other words, there is a decrease in the number of trainable candidates.

So, with the decline in graduation rates, there is a corresponding decrease in the number of black professionals. Why is this critical? Data demonstrates that blacks and Hispanics are more likely to practice in neighborhoods that need their services, and they are more likely to conduct research in areas impacting minority health concerns. (ETS, 2004) This makes their presence as professionals critical to the well-being of their respective groups. This is particularly important given reports that blacks are less likely to be referred to specialists for better treatment than whites.

Finally, blacks must succeed against great odds but that is not the end of their struggle. Even with higher levels of education than their white counterparts, they tend to earn less. For example, although black Hispanics tend to have higher levels of education than white Hispanics -- 12 years versus 11 years, respectively – the median income of white Hispanics is $5,000 higher than the median income of black Hispanics. (Fear, 2003) Additionally, black Hispanics tend to have higher rates of unemployment compared to white Hispanics. (Fears, 2003)

Dewayne Wickham, a *USA Today* columnist, points out that blacks with a college degree earn about the equivalent of whites who attend college but do not finish. (Wickham, 2003) He says that ". . . race appears to trump educational achievement." (Wickham, 2003) These are cogent reminders that blacks and whites do not live in similar worlds. Whiteness creates advantage in

America.   That advantage becomes more evident
after graduation.

K. Anthony Appiah demonstrates that even
for blacks who have "made it," there is a certain
fragility to life. He says, middle class blacks are not
as wealthy as middle class whites with the same
level of education; they tend to work in public
sector jobs that are easily threatened by downturns
in the economy; they depend upon the government
to enforce affirmative action standards; and they are
"twice as likely as their white counterparts to be
unemployed." (Appiah and Gutmann, 1996)

So, even with all the accoutrements of
success, blacks live a tenuous existence.   It is a
parallel universe. This is not to be mistaken for the
world of the athlete and the entertainer, which I will
address later.   I am speaking here of college
educated professionals who struggle against a "sea
of outrageous fortunes."

The facts indicate that although Americans
may all start closely ranked, things change as black
and Hispanic students progress toward the
workplace. The sad corollary is that the best efforts
sometimes end with blacks earning less than their
white counterparts even when they do all the right
things. We have to close these gaps and realize that
the gaps are not in the ability of the students but in
the system that prepares them for disparate
outcomes.

Chapter Four
The Color of Education

The whole belief in the concept of race is fabrication on a global scale. That time and discussion must be devoted to it is insufferable. Few people focus on the science of race rather than the sociology of race. Science has revealed what we have always known; race is farce. Sociology reveals that people believe race is real. There is no scientific, biological, anthropological or genetic basis for dividing humans into racial groups.

Race is not real. It is important not to miss this. "Race categories are social constructs; that is, concepts created from prevailing social perceptions without scientific evidence." (Witzig, 1996) The concept of race exists because we believe in it. "[D]ividing humans into 'races' and other invalid categories, and ranking the groups by intellectual capacity and human worth is still a practice that has not generated the outrage it deserves." (Hilliard, 2002) Scholarship has rendered any discussion of race as scientific fact moot.

Still, what is race? Race is a fraud that has been perpetrated on the world. It accounts for about .012% of our genetic material, miniscule to say the least. (Appiah and Gutmann, 1996) At best, it is a narrow window through which we see the external differences between humans. "Race . . . as a biological concept, picks out, at best, among humans, classes of people who share certain easily

68

observable physical characteristics, most notably skin, and a few visible features of the face and head." (Appiah and Gutmann, 1996) Here we already begin to see the problems of an attempt to be scientific about race. Its social significance is phenotypic rather than genotypic.

Race has no scientific basis. Race matters and persists in all its malignancy because people *believe* it is real. Phillip Kottak in his book *Anthropology: The Exploration of Human Diversity* (1991) points out that "The belief that races exist and are important is more common among the public than it is among biologists. Many Americans mistakenly believe that . . . races have a biological basis." To further add to the lunacy of a belief in race, most people labeled as black have a mixed heritage that is not usually evident on their faces.

According to K. Anthony Appiah, " . . . very large numbers (perhaps two-thirds of African-Americans have some European forebears; up to two-fifths have American Indian blood; and at least 5 percent of White Americans are thought to have African roots." (Appiah and Gutmann, 1996) ABC News reported that Wayne Joseph, a California man who believed he was black for more than fifty years, took a DNA test that found he was " . . . 57% Indo-European, 39% Native American, 4% East Asian, 0% African." (Wooten, 2003) This shocked even his mother. This really upsets the applecart. It makes the case race has no basis. Race is a social construct, based primarily on the false belief that color differences are more than skin deep.

However, it is belief, not science that keeps race around. It is the belief that people can be divided into races that creates this animus of difference. It is belief, a myth, not a fact. If that were the end of it, my book would end here; but the strength of a belief is enough to change history. How strong is belief? It was strong enough to cost nearly one million people their lives in the American Civil War. Belief was strong enough for D. W. Griffith's *The Birth of a Nation* (1915) to have sold out in American theaters despite its racist message. Belief was strong enough to cause perhaps 50 million black Africans to be sold into the most abominable form of slavery known to man in the Triangle of Trade – black lives for rum, sugar and tea. Belief was strong enough to make white parents stone black children on buses during the 1970s. I repeat – children. That belief is still strong enough to cause whites to flee neighborhoods where minorities move in. That belief caused America to convulse in the 1990s when Rodney King, O.J. Simpson, and James Byrd had their various troubles. Whites and blacks, and their respective sympathizers, chose sides. That same belief makes million dollar athletes and entertainers just as fearful of driving while black as it makes me. Belief, I tell you, is strong.

White people do not think of themselves in racial terms, nor does it consume their daily lives.

(Appiah and Gutmann, 1996) Blacks do not enjoy the privilege of being a-racial. "Unlike whites, black Americans cannot forget for one minute that they have a race; a race that links each individual black to the fate of every other black." (Appiah and Gutmann, 1996) There can be no discussion of education in America without some attempt to clarify this most ambiguous of terms.

Why does race matter in education? It is simple. Everything American is "tainted" and constructed upon a foundation of racism. David B. Wilkins, in his introduction to K. Anthony Appiah and Amy Gutmann's book *Color Conscious* (1996) puts it bluntly. He says, ". . . I understand that there has never been a moment in America's democratic experiment that has not been thoroughly tainted by racism and other forms of oppression." (Wilkins quoted in Appiah and Gutmann, 1996) In other words, if the root of the tree is racism, every limb, every branch and every leaf is infected. So, just as American politics, criminal justice, religion, housing, financial markets and voting are tainted, so is the American system of public education.

Race and education are tangled together in American history. Some of our most profound moments as a country have hinged on the interconnectedness of these two institutions. First, blacks were prohibited from formal education; but they endured through the founding of black schools and colleges, culminating in events like W.E.B. Dubois becoming the first black person to earn a

Ph.D. at Harvard University in sociology for his dissertation on *The Suppression of the African Slave Trade, 1638-1870.*

Second, throughout the period of segregation blacks endured and achieved another milestone in *Brown v. Board of Education of Topeka* (1954). This was a watershed moment. It did not end segregation but precipitated advances in all sectors of American life. Many cities did not end segregated schools until fifteen to twenty years after *Brown*, but there was a mandate for change. These mandates flowed into postsecondary education, employment, military, and other aspects of life. Brown did not solve racism in public education. Cities like Chicago, Boston and New York are still like tectonic plates shifting imperceptibly, threateningly but inevitably toward catastrophe over issues of race in public education.

Third, race and education are now tied in a life or death struggle in terms of whether black and minority children will receive a fair, equitable experience in the public education system. Race affects the flow of resources dispensed between schools; it controls who is appointed as administrators in schools; and its influence is present on school boards.

In particular, it is the persistent, belief that black and minority children are inferior that poses a threat in education. Some forty percent of school-age children are minorities. It does not take racism long to express itself in educational settings. Lisa

Delpit in her book *Other People's Children: Cultural Conflict in the Classroom* (1995) says that a "disconnect" has happens between white teachers and minority students and even between white teachers and their minority co-workers. However, the onus for this is not to be laid at the feet of teachers. Racism will exert influence in the public education system well into the 21st century. This is a truism that simply must be accepted.

Racism is in the curriculum. When your child attends a school where the curriculum speaks of the Founding Fathers of America but does not temper that discussion with the tragic truth that at least 20 of the men who signed the Declaration of Independence were slaveholders, Thomas Jefferson among them, that curriculum is false and inaccurate or, at least, misleading. Jefferson, whose resounding language we have admired and adored, was himself a racist. Let me pause to do away with the argument that he was a merely a man of his time.

Neither his enlightened idealism nor his Christianity was sufficient to make him adamant against the continuation of slavery. Listen to his own words, "I advance it as a suspicion only that the blacks whether originally a distinct race, or made distinct by time and circumstance, are inferior to the whites in the endowments of body and mind." (Jefferson, cited in Appiah and Gutmann, 1996) This would be the same man who is primarily responsible for the words, "We hold these truths to be self-evident that all men are created equal . . . ."

The only problem is that when Jefferson wrote the latter, he did not believe blacks to be in the human race, much less citizens of the new America.

Our children are not taught that European expansionism was a death knell to millions of blacks, Native Americans, Indians and other peoples around the world. The instability of modern day Africa is a legacy of the slavery and colonialism of Western Europe. Are children ever taught about the devastation of Aboriginal cultures in Australia and throughout the Pacific Basin? How about the plight of migrant workers? Our children still learn little if any thing about the great civilizations that existed before the Europeans unleashed their Doctrine of Manifest Destiny – the belief that their conquest of the world was God ordained.

Curriculum is an interesting field because it is the process by which we decide on what to teach (i.e., content) and how it will be taught (i.e., process). Content is the result of decisions that are made about what is to be included or left out of a course of study. The alternative to revising errors in American misstatement of world events has been to heighten the celebration of Black History Month, a time when the speeches of Dr. Martin Luther King, Jr. are replayed ad nauseum as if blacks have not accomplished anything lately.

Furthermore, the revision of American history in education is important for all children. Do whites not want their children to know about

Emmett Till? There is a very clear effort to minimize the ugliness in American history. America is not always at its best. Americans are eager for the children to know the horror of the Holocaust; but they shield them from American slavery and segregation.

Emmett Till, whose mother died in 2004, died at fourteen because of race prejudice. Yet, Emmett Till remains a footnote. It was the wretchedness of men killing a boy that helped to turn the tide in the struggle for Civil Rights. Every child should know his name. They should know Emmett because his death brought change despite the fact that his killers confessed to the crime in *Look Magazine* one year after being acquitted by an all white jury in sixty-eight minutes.

When slavery and segregation are taught in class, there is no depth, no probing, just a passing acknowledgement. Education must do more than that. Real teaching cannot be patronizing. I never hear the atrocities of the Holocaust tempered because we have people of German descent in our midst. Is that because it did not happen on American soil?

Here, I want to pose a seemingly simple question: if science has declared race a false notion, why does it still exist on every job application, the United States Census, and other important documents that you encounter? The American Anthropological Association (AAA) has asked for race to be removed from the Census. The Census

Bureau's response has been to further confuse people by telling them to check as many categories as apply. Surely, if scientists cannot decide about race, how can the average citizen remotely understand the concept? What does the biracial child do? As a matter of fact, biracial has become a whole new category of persons. Again, the insanity persists. Eventually, we will follow the insanity of Brazil which has more than 500 designations for race. (Kottak, 1991)

Furthermore people do not understand that race and ethnicity are not the same. Race is a color designation that exists for no purpose other than to distinguish groups into superior and inferior. "Ultimately, race as an ideology about human beings, was subsequently spread from Europe to other parts of the world. It became a strategy for dividing, ranking and controlling colonized people used by colonial powers everywhere." (Quotation from the American Anthropological Association at www.aaanet.org) Clearly race was contrived and exists to this day for purposes of control.

Ethnicity, on the other hand, concerns one's historical, heritage, cultural and language connections. I did mention earlier that there are more than one million black Hispanics in America. By appearance, their skin may be dark; but linguistically, Spanish is their first language. Because of the burden that race carries, many have divested themselves of any notion of blackness and embraced their Hispanic heritage. This is the case for some. Then, there are others who laude their Afro-Hispanic heritage through music, literature and history. My point here, though, is that a lack of understanding of race and ethnicity further demonstrates that race should not matter.

In my own case, I found a conundrum in my family tree. I attended a family reunion recently where an older cousin gave me a picture of my great grandfather. I was stunned to look at his picture and see my own nose and eyes. However, I was more stunned when my cousin informed me that that my great grandfather was Hispanic. No one had ever shared this with me. It took a little while to get my mind around this. So, now what am I to do with the next Census? I think I'll check all the boxes!

Racism is allowed to persist because it is as important to the structure of our society as government. All of our policies toward the rest of the world are influenced by the fact that America – a predominantly white country – believes itself to be superior to other nations. We teach it to our children. We are more privileged but not better. It is arrogant racism that has led us to war in Afghanistan and Iraq, not largesse for the people of these countries. We believe our way of life is best, that it produces the best kind of society. Hence, our wars are really marketing tools to take America's belief system abroad.

It is important to understand that racism is about power. It not just the ability to look disfavorably or condescendingly at someone else.

That is prejudice. Prejudice and racism are not identical. It is that ability to gain advantage through a system that actualizes power into an advantage over another group that sets racism apart from prejudice. (Tatum, 1997) Black folk and minorities do not have this power – particularly in America. (Tatum, 1997)

White people want to deflect attention from racism by saying that blacks can be prejudiced, but I don't know of a group of black people anywhere in America who can – of their own accord – force their will upon whites. Perhaps whites do not feel this power in a personal way but they certainly do reap its benefits in a systemic sense. (Tatum, 1997) To make it simple, there is not a white person in America who would trade places with his "black" friend.

This provides another reason for the interconnectivity of education and race. Whites make no effort to understand the dynamics of how racism unfolds within the culture because nothing in their life experience requires them to take on such knowledge. Furthermore, they have no intention of assuming guilt for racism if it can be avoided. Dr. Beverly D. Tatum, president of Spelman College, raises an interesting point. She says that racism is so powerful that it negates the American idea of a meritocracy. (Tatum, 1997)

I would go a step further to add that the systemic racism of America creates two parallel worlds. While whites may live in a meritocracy, black people's parallel world is a "raceocracy." In the "raceocracy," you can do the equivalent of your white counterpart but get less for the same effort. For example, if you take a black person and a white person and they both get the same level of education, the results will be markedly different and not just because of personal effort. K. Anthony Appiah makes this plain when he talks about the disparity of wealth between white and middle class achievements and lifestyles. (Appiah and Gutmann, 1996)

Recently, I was confronted by an African-American man at the barber shop who tried to convince me that black people can achieve anything they desire in America. He tried to drive home the point that racism is not a deterrent to success for black Americans. I, conversely, asserted my "raceocracy" theory that a black and white person could do the same things but get different results.

This brings me to another problem of perception and reality. While whites may not want to accept that racism creates a privileged existence for which they are passive beneficiaries, blacks often want to deny or ignore racism's limiting effects. As it concerns education, black and minority children are impacted by race because it creates a parallel dimension that they travel through in urban, inner city schools where all the accoutrements of equality seem to be there, but the result is two distinct and unequal educational experiences.

This happens in education because it happens in every other aspect of life in America. In criminal justice, blacks and whites get different sentences for the same crimes. Blacks and whites apply for loans and the white person's chances for approval are better. Blacks and whites go to college and whites advance further and get higher salaries with the same level of education. Blacks and whites can drive, but only blacks are profiled as prone to criminal behavior and are subjected to Driving While Black (DWB) policing. Dr. Tatum summarizes this parallel existence beautifully. She says, "Despite the current rhetoric about affirmative action and 'reverse racism,' every social indicator, from salary to life expectancy, reveals the advantage of being white." (Tatum, 1997)

W.E.B. Dubois looked into the future of America in 1903 and saw what most Americans did not – that racism would remain relevant. Most black people would like to be free of the burden that race creates. It is an albatross about the neck, an asphyxiating poison that lingers in the air. What would any of the great figures of history (e.g., Langston Hughes, Richard Wright, Gwendolyn Brooks, Arna Bontempts, Claude McKay) think about the state of things. I wonder whether they would think we had squandered an opportunity. Clearly, change has happened; but the change has not always been productive?

Perhaps the thing that troubles me the most is that I hear black people constantly talking about being afraid when they confront racial injustice. Fear is an affront when denigration, dogs and death were the calling cards of our Forefathers. Our Forefathers were not the white men in Independence Hall in 1787 who argued over drafts of a national Constitution that would not guarantee freedom to black slaves, Native Americans, Latinos or Asians. Our Forefathers – slaves and underpaid immigrants -- were the men and women who slaved for no money, picked cotton and tobacco in the South and fruit and vegetables in the West, built railroads and bridges and had no say, not even for themselves.

They were fearless people. They did not faint or die. They worked through slavery, segregation, economic exploitation, murder and rape. No one has built a monument to them or laid alabaster pillars in their honor. Homage ought to be paid to them on a scale as grand as the Washington, Jefferson or Lincoln memorials.

So, black people cannot be afraid. If adults cower before the circumstances, should not our children surrender to failure? We are 147 years removed from the Supreme Court declaring Dred Scott property rather than a person. We are 141 years removed from the Emancipation Proclamation and 136 years removed from the 13th Amendment that ended slavery for good. We are 108 years removed from Homer Plessy's humiliation. We are 50 years removed from *Brown*. We are forty years removed from the March on Washington, the Civil

Rights Act of 1964 and the Voting Rights Act of 1965, documents that were required to reinforce our right to enjoy the basic privileges of work, housing and the franchise. Why should we be afraid at all?

Minorities have no room for fear, just better preparation. That we have endured these things and free education goes unclaimed is criminal and sinful. Sin is both acts committed and those omitted. Every time we omit study, we sin. Every time an assignment is given in school and our children do not return it, we sin. Every college scholarship that is not claimed represents a sin against the Creator and our ancestors. The opportunity for education should be precious to blacks, Native Americans and Hispanics.

I do not understand the abject dislike and disconnection that black children have with education. I understand the hindrances of high mobility, and I have seen the ravages of a drug culture that has left a whole generation bereft of parents only to be raised by grandparents or themselves. Perhaps it is this lack of an intergenerational connection that has led to black children being unconcerned. When I walk into schools that are majority black or Hispanic and there is no fire in students to get out of poverty, I am at a loss. Susan Black writes, "Student disengagement occurs at all levels – in fact, some first graders I observed have as much apathy toward learning as many 10th graders." (Black, 2003)

There is this animus of expecting instant success rather than success earned by hard work.

Blacks and Hispanics must realize that there is no room for apathy toward education. America will have its poor; it prefers them in shades of black and brown. The American meritocracy is skewered in favor of whites. They reserve privileges to themselves and foster poor preparation for minorities. Randall Robinson says, "I've come to accept . . . that the squirreling away of privilege by a pampered few . . . is largely made possible and facilitated by the poor and provincial public education that the [P]resident tolerates for the many." (Robinson, 2004)

Robinson understands the breath and scope of racial dysfunction and its perpetuation by poor intellectual development. Blacks and Hispanics must rekindle a collaborative spirit that dates back to efforts to throw off colonialism. After Haiti threw off the French, it proceeded to assist fledgling revolutionaries in South America (e.g., Simon Bolivar). Blacks and Hispanics have worked together in the past. Hopefully, there will be no under the table trade offs on either side that amount to betrayal. Whites are savvy. They undo allegiances against them by offering favors to one minority group or the other. Right now, they are courting Hispanics with the hope of undermining the interests of American blacks.

Race is important in education for another reason – the end result. By that, I mean whether our children graduate or not. Each year, 1.2 million 18 years olds drop out of school with no diploma. (*USA Today*, March 31, 2004) When you consider that a large segment of these are black and minority children, who are the products of a failed system, and not failures themselves, you can see that the repercussions of racism in education are staggering. I challenge black and minority families to nurture a in our children a love for learning. We owe it to those who have struggled and who are struggling.

Chapter Five
A Parallel Universe

America was supposed to be a "melting pot" according to J. Hector St. John de Crevecoeur, who made that assertion about a new America whose citizens were white and very recently European. (Maharidge, 1993) His exact quote was "Here individuals of all nations are melted into one race of men." (St. John quoted in Maharidge, 1993) Of course, St. John was speaking only of Europeans, who saw themselves as different peoples, nations or cultures but not races in the sense of color.

The word race has not always been used exclusively to refer to a group's color. J. Hector St. John de Crevecoeur was not speaking of Native Americans. He was not speaking at all of Africans held in slavery. The America he perceived was one in which Europeans, who saw themselves as distinct cultural groups, were losing their European identities in lieu of a new Americanized one. Even now, being Americanized usually means divesting oneself of cultural or racial distinctions and adopting the attitudes of condescension and superiority that make Americans despised.

Over the years, St. John's melting pot analogy was wrongfully adopted to suggest that America was the perfect place to become a part of something new, something American, a place where color or ethnicity does not matter. The problem with St. John's view of America was that he did not include Asians, Native-Americans, Hawaiians or Africans in that idealized, futuristic melting pot.

This self-absorbed world view is typical of Europeans and later Americans who seem to conceptualize the world in the absence of people it does not deem relevant – namely, people of color or people in the fictional Third World. We saw this in 1994 when Rwanda lost some 800,000 of its citizens in 100 days while Euro-America watched in silence. This carnage could only happen because African lives were less valuable on the world stage than those of Balkans. This concept alone bespeaks the condescending nature of the Euro-American world view and contravenes the obvious fact that the world is predominantly populated by people of color. Even America is predicted to undergo a "browning" by 2050.

However, the Southern Hemisphere of the world -- full of brown and black people -- will ultimately demand attention because ". . . 95% of all population growth between now and the year 2025 will occur in the underdeveloped Southern Hemisphere." (Maharidge, 1993) Due to economic concerns, poverty and overcrowding, this population growth will spill over into Europe and the North America and increase the pressures on our changing social construct. (Maharidge, 1993) At some point, roles will reverse. When the Third World belches forth its teeming millions, Europe and America will get sick.

In my view, people of African descent –
whether they be African, Afro-Iraqi, Afro-Hispanic
Afro-Caribbean or African-American -- are still
very much outside that melting pot as ever. Blacks
will never melt into America as long as the first
thing people see is their color and the next thing
they think is inferior. I am sure that this postulation
will make some blacks and whites uncomfortable,
but the truth is for most blacks in America, the
quality of life they live compared to the majority of
Americans is different.

I believe not "melting" has been a good
thing. "Collective identities have a tendency . . . to
'go imperial,' dominating not only people of other
identities, but the other identities, whose shape is
exactly what makes each of us what we individually
and distinctively are." (Appiah and Gutmann, 1996)
In other words, Americanism can be its own form of
tyranny. All is not lost when you don't conform.

The amazing thing is that in spite of the
pressure to homogenize, the evidence of the black
identity shows up everywhere in America. Our
music has been copied and "covered" for
generations. For example, Pat Boone's sanitized
version of Little Richard's risque tune "Tooty
Fruity was a blanched as his trademark shoes."
When I watch the likes of Britney Spears imitate
Janet Jackson's moves or N' Sync recreate the teen
sensationalism of New Edition, I can see that we are
at least accounted for. The rapper Eminem, whose
talents are at least evident, owes his rap virtuosity to

black artists like Dr. Dre who helped to mold him into a phenomenon among suburban white kids. Of course, Karl Kani, Phat Farm, FUBU, Sean Jean and other black fashion labels have helped to make urban street wear both marketable and hip.

Yet, none of these things have helped to close the divide in the quality of life many young black and Hispanic people are faced with growing up in the inner cities of America. Black children suffer from a brand of social malaise that makes them indifferent to learning but passionate about material things. Blacks are approximately 20% of students nationally. Hispanics have surpassed blacks in the general population as of the 2000 Census; however, they also surpassed blacks in public schools in 1998. (Zehr, 2004) Gary Orfield intimates that Hispanics are ". . . the most segregated by both race and poverty." (Orfield, 2001) Still, blacks and Hispanics have common ground. Their lives are filled with decrepit neighborhoods, where schools are old and technologically deficient, and where violence and death are as common as the trash that lines the streets.

Hispanic parents in Chicago had to resort to a hunger strike for nineteen days to force school officials to build a new school for their children. (Zehr, 2004) This is a shame in a city where Hispanics are more than one-third of the students in the school district. (Zehr, 2004) Is this the kind of action that is required when 90% of the students attending the school will be poor rather than middle class? (Zehr, 2004) This is decidedly unpleasant when one considers that we are spending more than $100 billion dollars on a war in which black and Hispanics are dying for freedom in Iraq. In *Quitting America* (2004), Randall Robinson calls this: the poor killing the poor for the benefit of the rich.

There is no melting when your neighborhood is predominantly black or Hispanic or your reservation is completely Native-American. These groups live in -- I say again -- a parallel world, one marked by drug addiction, low achievement, and hopelessness. They live in a world where every privilege is earned and none is given freely. That Hispanic parents should have to resort to a hunger strike to get a school raises questions about America.

I doubt that whites can relate to the sense of urgency one of the Hispanic parents in Chicago felt who said "Education is everything . . . I didn't have a good one." (Zehr, 2004) For poor communities, education still represents a way out. The poor continue to place their hope in public education to move each generation up the social scale. This is a necessary hope in communities where so much else is lacking.

Liberty City in Miami, Florida became a bastion of death in the 1980's and 1990's when crack cocaine and AIDS erased a whole generation. Miami was almost like Egypt of the Old Testament when the Death Angel roamed and cries could be heard from mothers whose children were snatched by premature death. My cousin Red was a dope dealer. He used to come by the house and brag about his money. He was young, handsome and respectful to my parents. Red was shot gangland-style. His body bullet-riddled was found under a bridge. At his funeral, people fancied the gold his "boys" laid on his dead body before it was put in the ground. Red died in his twenties.

How about Tammy? The last time I saw Tammy was in Liberty City. We had grown up in church. She was "tricking." I spoke to her and asked why and what for. She said, "Do you want to date or what?" Tammy died of an overdose in a crack den one week later. She might have been twenty.

Then, I still remember looking into the dying eyes of Chris. He had grown up in church, become a preacher, sung powerfully to the Lord and died of AIDS in his 30s. I will never forget looking into his eyes which seemed so large and desperate one last time. I knew that I would never see him again. I could not go to his funeral. It simply hurt too much. Does this sound like the America that you know or want to melt into? This is the parallel world of poor people, be they white black or some other minority.

This is why whites build walls and plant beautiful flowers and name their communities wonderful, calming names such as *Summer Winds*. "They believe they can shut out the urban nightmare, something like a passenger on the Titanic feeling secure in a locked stateroom." (Maharidge, 1993) When I ride through these neighborhoods, I am aware that more is going on than just a beautification project. There is a conscious effort to carve out a high-priced existence apart from blacks and Hispanics.

Many people do not know the history of planned communities and restrictive covenants. The original intent of these communities was that residents conspired to prevent minorities from moving into their neighborhoods by requiring that the association had a right of first refusal to buy back any home that was to be sold. Hence, blacks and minorities could be excluded without allusions to races or minorities in the legal documents. There was a tacit understanding that exclusion was the goal.

The United States Census for 2000 demonstrates that our diversity is marred by a high degree of racial separation in residential housing patterns. "The average non-Hispanic white person continues to live in a neighborhood that looks very different from those neighborhoods where the average black, Hispanic or Asian lives. The average white person in metropolitan America lives in a neighborhood that is 80% white and only 7% black . . . Residential segregation among blacks and whites remains high in cities and in suburbs around the country." (Logan, 2001) There has been no significant or "net" change in Hispanic segregation from whites since 1980 despite their radical growth within the general American population. (Logan, 2001)

In fact, segregation levels remain about the same as 1960. Even with more affluent blacks, neighborhood segregation reinforces the disparity in income with blacks only earning about 70% the income of their white middle class peers. A number of things coalesce together with these residential schisms. Social mobility, earning power, and access to quality of education are all impacted by where a person lives.

It is no surprise that the housing and education disparities that lead to depthless poverty inspire little empathy from whites. They have developed a lifelong insensitivity to the suffering that not sharing the wealth creates. America is proud of its accumulation of things; this is supported by a sense of entitlement to all things superior – even if at the expense of others within their midst. (Robinson, 2004) Whites refuse to solve problems generated by color prejudice and demonstrate recalcitrance in refusing to discuss the question. (Appiah and Gutmann, 1996) Then, they secure the support of well-healed blacks such as Ward Connerly, Shelby Steele, John McWhorter or the like to go on national television to confirm their unjust actions.

Hence, the question of two distinct spheres of existence will come as a surprise to no one. White Americans live amidst privilege and security while their minority counterparts live on the verge of bankruptcy and unemployment. This is the parallel universe I want to address.

America was built at the expense of millions of Native-American, Hawaiian and African lives. Americans imbibe these unearned benefits with no remorse. Whoever gives up privilege voluntarily? I am more concerned that they turn a blind eye to inner cities where people stew in poverty and violence that will eventually assault the painted, ivy covered walls of their exclusionary communities. Housing differences lead to disparate educational experiences for our children.

Race plays a part in where people choose to live. Housing patterns clearly show this. One thing is certain. Whites do not want to live with minorities. John A. Powell (1999) makes this point cogently when he writes:

> Race plays a significant role in creating and maintaining fragmented metropolitan regions through urban sprawl and racialized, concentrated poverty . . . I have argued that one of the central forces behind the sprawl explosion is white aversion to blacks . . .
> One cannot adequately account for the increase in racial segregation . . . by simply examining personal choice, personal racial dynamics or market forces.

Powell states here that housing segregation is not coincidental. Whites are not moving just because they prefer beautiful communities. Powell also said that "Jobs relocated to the suburbs, and the central city's strong tax base soon followed. It was no coincidence that these shifts occurred shortly after large numbers of blacks moved into these urban areas. The fracturing of metropolitan areas is almost always a racially motivated method of excluding blacks. In order for this racial sorting to work, however, suburbs had to both attract whites and exclude blacks." (Powell, 1999)

Whites move because they do not want to live next door to people they deem unsuitable. As Miami's population swelled from predominantly white to predominantly Hispanics from 1950 to 1990, whites all but abandoned Miami-Dade and moved to Broward and Palm Beach counties. (Dunn, 1997) They did it with help from favorable governmental policies. This is not new. "In recent history, affirmative action for whites, motivated by racially restrictive housing policies that helped 15 million white families procure homes with FHA loans from the 1930's through the 1960's, while people of color were mostly excluded from these same programs." (Wise, 2003)

Whites are deliberate and systematic in their racism. When they need to achieve a goal, they develop policies to support their objective. These policies, which include greater access to home loans and the creation of vouchers and charter schools, help them to move into neighborhoods with new, non-minority schools. This demonstrates that racism is systemic.

When you ask any white person about being racist, those with a modicum of grace will deny it. Most are not in the extreme sense; but when it comes to threatening their benefit system, most will choose sides – the white side. This selfish and malevolent disposition is the origin of their vehemence against school desegregation, affirmative action, fair labor practices and other attempts to balance the scales. *Whites know it is good to be white in America. They won't give up that privilege without a fight.* They are not afraid to be passive recipients of administrative and policy decisions that yield unspoken benefits to their group. They have no desire to integrate.

Tim Wise notes white people's indifference to their unmerited favor by writing that they ". . . strike the pose of self-sufficiency while ignoring the advantages [they] have been afforded in every realm of activity: housing, education, employment, criminal justice, politics, banking and business." (Wise, 2003) All these areas indicate points where whites receive greater opportunity than blacks or Hispanics; and it is that entrée that serves as the backdrop to an existence that minorities can only dream of. Wise goes on to say that these opportunities have become completely matter-of-fact in the lives of whites, ". . . like water to the fish . . . ." (Wise, 2003)

By choice, most white people do not see that this separation is engendering a dual system of living. Richard Kahlenberg -- although I do not agree with his premise of creating middle class schools -- registered a ringing plea for change in his book *All Together Now: Creating Middle Class Schools and Public Choice* (2001). Kahlenberg says, "[t]he failure to educate poor children adequately also means crime and welfare dependency and reduced future earnings." (Kahlenberg, 2001) He asserts that gaps in student achievement later translate into a diminution in life chances and a decrease in the ability to move up the social scale.

He writes, "[a]bout 70% of Americans stay in the same socioeconomic class into which they were born; the children of poorly educated parents make up just 2% of the professional and managerial class." (Kahlenberg, 2001) The schism in public education is breeding another class of poor students with a limited outlook. Their mobility is limited and their potential level of achievement is specious.

More than 90% of eligible school-aged students in America attend public schools. (Kahlenberg, 2001) Even if there was a desire to reconstitute our educational structure, it must take into account where people live. Richard Kahlenberg's model of "middle-class" schools is a great idea whose major flaw is that whites live in nearly exclusive communities. Moreover, they are building charter schools within those communities which further isolate white children from their minority peer group.

The point that I am trying for is this. If 80% of white students do not attend schools with minority children (Orfield, 2001) and if whites live in neighborhoods that are 80% white (Logan, 2001), where is the melting? It is interesting that these two numbers are identical. On a deeper level, they connote that the whole notion of a melting pot is a myth for minorities. Blacks and Hispanics remain isolated residentially and educationally. The question, then, is what does this separation spawn within our communities?

In South Texas it has spawned a series of shanty communities next to "McMansions," where rich whites live adjacent to their Hispanic neighbors. (Relin, 2004) Listen to this description. "Shantytowns known as 'colonias' are as common in this part of South Texas as fields of cabbage and sugarcane. More than 500,000 people live in the area's 1,500 unincorporated communities, where running water is scarce, electricity is a luxury and one in every two children endures hunger." (Reline, 2004) This is a quintessential example of the parallel universe. Can you image the difference in the quality of life the "colonias" versus the "McMansions." Can you imagine the difference in education?

In the absence of clear evidence to the contrary, I would have thought this was a description of a Third World country. Yet, how many times in America is this scene repeated? I wonder does this move anyone in America but me? Dr. Beverly Daniel Tatum (1997) reminds us in *Why Are All the Black Kids Sitting Together in the Cafeteria?"* that there is no incentive to change this because it means that the dominant group would have to relinquish some of its privileges. Furthermore, ". . . dominant groups do not like to be reminded of the existence of inequality." (Tatum, 1997) This is a sad commentary on the privileged of America.

The critical thing here is that we must see where the trail of separation leads. It leads to poverty. There are some 34 million persons in poverty in America; 13 million of them are children. (Relin, 2004) We cannot turn our eyes from this crisis. The poor sit within eyeshot of the rich in America. These worlds are close but they never touch.

While there may be many factors that can effect change to these circumstances, no institution is more important to the reform of America's racial, ethnic and economic apartheid than our system of education. This reminds me of something. We keep saying that our children are the most important resource we have. Yet, we pay teachers a negligible sum for being the caretakers of that future.

I had the opportunity to attend my very first professional basketball game in 2004. I was invited to sit in a luxury box and take in the game from the quiet of this area. I was amazed by the quality of the treatment people received in these rooms – food, wine, etc. As I settled in and began to concentrate on the game, I watched professional basketball players miss more shots than they made. I wondered why these men were paid as much as $14 million dollars a year for being 40% successful at their work.

I began to juxtaposition this non-essential social function against the profession of teaching. A teacher I know ran across my mind, and I thought of a conversation she had with me. She is the mother of three children and a single parent. Her salary was about $45,000 annually. She had also just lost some of that disposable income to a change in district health insurance, leading to an additional monthly expenses to cover her children. By the way, she is by far the best teacher in her school and perhaps the best I have ever met.

As I watched the basketball game with its well-heeled but poor shooting millionaires, it dawned on me that we really did not care about children because we pay their teachers considerably less than we pay men playing a boy's game. There is a scripture that says a man's heart is where his treasures are. In other words, you know what we cherish by what we spend our money on. Judging from what we spend on education, we do not care about teachers and we care even less about children.

Separate and unequal living conditions lead to separate and unequal educational experiences. Unequal educational experiences lead to unequal job opportunities. Unequal jobs lead to unequal earning power. Unequal earning power leads to vast disparities in the quality of life. Every city that I have visited has this dichotomy apparent in its population demographic. There is a magnificent opulence juxtaposed to abject poverty. Again, when the two groups of children emerge from their respective schools and enter college or enter the workplace, who do you think comes out on top?

I wonder why we cannot find the will to be fair? The American way is to possess as much as possible and to allow children to go hungry and live in conditions of poverty. I visited St. Louis, Missouri several years ago. I was living next to the great arch. I was in awe. From my hotel window, I could see East St. Louis. Near the end of my trip, I drove across to take a closer look. As I drove through the area, I nearly shed tears at the wheel because of the stark difference between St. Louis and East St. Louis.

The devastation and poverty that I saw was breathtaking. I drove back to my hotel stunned and deflated about the whole trip. I will never forget that visit. What I saw was this parallel existence: one world white and wealthy, another black and impoverished. When I compare my St. Louis experience with South Texas, I see two worlds a world apart.

The crux of the problem is that residential segregation leads to differing qualities of education. There is a close connection between levels of poverty and the quality of schools students attend. Blacks and Hispanics attend schools with higher rates of poverty. (Logan, 2002) With poverty comes a host of problems like poor health and poor quality teachers, less technologically sound school buildings and low quality education; and since blacks and Hispanics are present in large number in these schools, they pay the price of being separated. (Logan, 2002) "Separate means unequal in America public schools. Schools vary greatly in their class composition, and many studies indicate that a disproportionate concentration of poverty in any one school undermines educational achievement for all students in that school." (Logan, 2002)

We must speak frankly here. We cannot continue to say the fate of minority children is the result of their poor performances on standardized tests without taking into account the forces that bring them to a point of failure. If you took white children and placed them under the burden of poverty, gave them poor housing conditions and gave them poor quality teachers who had low expectations about their abilities, is there any doubt that their results on standardized tests would begin to lag? Why do we tolerate this for minority children? Children cannot be held accountable for the nefarious doings of adults.

Americans must understand that this cultivation of an underclass will ultimately undermine our effort to remain at the forefront of the globalization movement. In fact, America is breeding a discontented and disaffected generation whose rage will vent itself inside our borders. Need I remind anyone of the close connection between criminal behavior and poor education? There is not enough mortar and bricks available to insulate the well educated and the wealthy from the flood of poorly educated minority youth who will roam our streets in future generations.

Racial separation demonstrates that we are an immature people. I can remember all the talk of solidarity that followed the September 11th tragedy. I remember watching on television as politicians, pundits and professors spoke of the renewed sense of oneness that allegedly pervaded the country. I knew that once all the emotion of the moment ran its course, these same people would return to the splendor of their separate neighborhoods and the security of their separate and unequal worlds.

I am inclined to say that we learned nothing from the New York calamity. The whole September 11th imbroglio was born in hatred. That hatred was nurtured in the cloisters of racial and ethnic isolation. This made it easy for one group to devalue the lives of 3,000 American citizens. This in turn inspired the devaluation of lives in Afghanistan and Iraq.

Living apart creates divides in the mind and in the spirit. More than anything, it creates misperceptions. It is easier to mistreat *them*. These misperceptions are at the heart of very conscious decisions to allow black and Hispanic children to be perceived as unteachable or not worth teaching. When minority schools contain few or no white children, those schools are neglected and policies are allowed to continue such as placing poorly qualified teachers in those schools. This is done even though we know that "[s]egregation translates to very different school experiences for children of different racial and ethnic backgrounds." (Logan, 2002)

The heart of this matter is that we must live up to our words. Yet, there is no evidence in the American historical record that we have the will to do what's right. When one surveys the history of America, it is clear that whites want to co-exist with blacks and minorities at a distance, and they do not want to live next door or go to school with minorities.

Chapter Six
Educational Policies That Discriminate

The disgraceful state of public education is the result of sound planning. *It fails at its mission to provide skills and competence to a significant segment of minority students because that is what it is meant to do.* Quality education is for the privileged; miseducation and indoctrination is for the poor. Despite all the altruistic talk about equal educational opportunities for all children and despite the best efforts of well-meaning educators who have striven to make bricks without straw, public education bears all the trappings of a fixed fight.

We knew this as soon as we understood how *Brown v. Board of Education* (1954) was to be administered. *Brown* was subverted from the start. It could not be successful on its own. Brown probably has had a greater impact outside public education than inside. While there was a strong public impression that equality public education was at hand, it was clear that the government had no intention of enforcing the spirit of the case.

In Miami, Florida, for example, *Brown* was not fully enforced until the 1970s. Initial attempts to implement *Brown* at Orchard Villa Elementary school led to immediate white flight. (Dunn, 1997) Since the second *Brown* case slowed integration and federal judges limited its reach to urban centers, the case lost its teeth. For the most part, whites didn't put up much of a fight. They sold their homes and fled to the suburbs, built new schools, and left the aging inner-city infrastructures of minorities.

Miami sought to further diffuse the tenets of *Brown* by instituting the magnet concept – that is, turning inner-city schools into specialty and college preparatory centers. Magnates were Miami's way of patronizing the federal desegregation mandate. The plan was for whites to voluntarily choose to attend predominantly minority schools. In no way, did they intend to fully comply with the spirit of the order.

White and Hispanic teachers were transferred into black schools but very few classrooms were integrated at the student level. That portion of the order could not be complied with simply because there were not very many white children left to move. Their parents had, like whites in numerous other cities, moved them beyond the reach of *Brown*. The goal – successfully done I might add – was to frustrate the intent of *Brown*. With later influxes of Hispanics in the 1980s, Miami became a majority-minority school district.

Miami Northwestern, my former high school, was still 100% black when I graduated in 1979. Except for a few students in the magnet program in 2004, the school is still predominantly black. According to the Miami-Dade County Public Schools 2002-03 *District and School Profiles,* Miami Northwestern in 91% black, 7% Hispanic,

2% Asian/Indian and 0% white. Across the nation, even schools that were at the heart of the desegregation battle are now in pretty much the same predicament.

Miami is indicative of the state of affairs in public education in America's inner cities. Despite its position as the fourth largest school district in the nation, it is a predominantly minority school district -- some 90% -- according to its 2002-03 *Statistical Abstract*. Whites represent approximately 10% of Miami-Dade County students. This is strange in a county that was once predominantly white 40 years ago. This pattern also emulates the national trend of re-segregation that has occurred within the last thirty years.

Two significant events led to this demographic configuration: white flight after Brown and white flight after the 1980 Cuban Boat Flotilla. Miami is the consummate mirror of the American dilemma in public education of whites preferring to live in communities that are 80% white and attending schools that are 80% or more white. While not created overtly by law, *de jure* segregation is very much at work here.

De jure segregation exists because whites who fled Miami were given incentives to do so. They fled Miami to West Broward County and to Palm Beach County, just north of Miami These communities are awash in charter and newly built public schools so that their children do not have to attend school with minority children for the most part.

It should also be noted that this occurred while there was a standing order for desegregation issued by the late federal Judge C. Clyde Atkins. However, there were other forces at work. The federal government throughout the 1980s and 1990s refused to enforce long-standing desegregation orders and sent the signal that, for all practical purposes, national support for legally enforced desegregation had ended.

Now, we must deal with the question of *de facto* segregation – that is, segregation which results from circumstances rather than law. Is there some benefit in school jurisdictions that are predominantly minority? Certainly, when a district is heavily minority it increases the likelihood, if not the demand, for minority administrators. In the case of Miami, the decrease of whites in Miami gave rise to Johnny Jones, the first African-American superintendent, and later to Joe Fernandez, a Hispanic superintendent. As things stand today, Hispanics are approximate 65% of the population of Miami and blacks about 20%.

So, two minority groups, in essence have virtual control of the district. Actually, Hispanics have a lopsided majority in the student population, the county at large and on the nine member School Board. Blacks are outnumbered 3:1 in the general population and 2:1 in the student population. Whites are a minority in Miami. That will shock some across the country.

However, there is an inherent danger in such relationships. There is the danger the whites may be subject to discrimination. Also, blacks, who are soundly outnumbered, also find themselves in the precarious posture of being at the mercy of the larger Hispanic minority group. The trouble with such a predicament is to whom could a complaint for discrimination be addressed when the majority is a minority? The question now is will the minorities be fair to one another? While the whites are away, how will the minorities play?

Miami has an opportunity to do some great things, but I am not certain that school district officials have the will to do it. For example, during the early 1990s, black Ph.D. candidates who were better qualified were repeatedly passed over as candidates for superintendent. Moreover, qualifications for the superintendency were reduced from doctoral to master level degrees in a blatant effort to include marginally qualified candidates who eventually won the job in succession. The latter of the two under-qualified superintendents failed and was fired.

Miami, then, made an unconventional move, hiring Merrett Stierheim, a white former city and county manager, after a series of scandals that caused the public to question the integrity of the School Board and the qualifications of the superintendent. The superintendent prior to

Stierheim was shown to have acquired his masters degree from a then dubious program out of the University of Northern Colorado. The degree was allegedly earned in about eight weekends rather than the standard two year period.

Stierheim, though an anomaly because he had no prior experience in the field of public education, represented a national trend toward bifurcating the duties of running the business of the district and the overseeing of the classroom aspect under a Chief Academic Officer. This has taken place in San Diego, Seattle, Washington, D.C., and New York City. Other unconventional tactics on the national level included cities like New York and Chicago placing the selection of the superintendent under the direction of the mayor's office -- thus, further politicizing an already highly political office.

The real unanswered question here is what about the children? This is a question that seldom seems to make its way to the forefront in discussions about what will happen to public education. Children are not at the center of decision-making in public education. The same selfishness that drives Washington politics drives local school allocations of resources. The best qualified seldom win and seldom make decisions that are in the interest of children.

Another more lethal policy decision concerns the implementation of state assessments on a national scale. Approximately 48 of 50 states have adopted such tests to determine everything from school grading criteria to pupil progression. It is in this latter area that minority students are disproportionately impacted -- another case of de facto discrimination. That is, more minority students are being held back in third grade at greater rates, delayed or prevented from graduating and, in some cases, being prevented from entering college as a result of standardized tests.

One of the most important but least talked about problems is that standardized tests raise more questions than they answer. These tests rely on a "one-size-fits–all" approach. (Hilliard, 2003) Any keen observer knows that humans are hardly carbon copies. No two are alike. "Standardization in testing and assessment is of high value to entrepreneurs (i.e., test makers) who make money, if they mass produce products such as tests . . . Unfortunately, humanity is made up of a plurality of cultures." (Hilliard 2003)

Hilliard's point here is that any attempt at standardization is fraught with the potential for over extrapolation. There is no standard human. Every attempt at standardization in testing is a guess; and in some cases, it's not even a good one. Perhaps this is at the core of the problem in New York City where some 10,000 third grade students may be held back, surpassing the 4,800 held back in 2003. (*USA Today*, June 4, 2004) Unfortunately, children bear the brunt of grand educational experiments such as state assessments.

Standards are questionable. "There is no standard language or standard culture. There is no standard curriculum. Even if there were such a thing, that children learn differently and express that learning differently through their own cultural prisms belies the notion that a test can accurately tell you about the child's capability for life." (Hilliard, 2003) In other words, testing is a flawed process with more political than educational ends. The more important problem with testing is that it is but another tool rife with the imprimatur of supremacist ideology. This has led to a host of "invalid and bad practices in testing and assessment. . . ." (Hilliard, 2003) A standard is a mold, something most people rarely fit.

Although states have tried to mitigate the damage for political reasons (i.e., too many students not graduating is political suicide), there is nothing that can erase the fact that a student who has gone through twelve years of school is held accountable for not being able to pass a single test, even if his or her grades indicate adequate progress. In Texas, for example, this has led to increased dropout rates. However, my point of contention is a bit different.

I cited a set of circumstances earlier that make testing a form of double jeopardy. Black and minority children are at the mercy of teachers who tend to be less experienced, who are certified less often, and who have lower expectations for students. (Haycock 2003; Hrabowski, 2003) Additionally, experienced teachers prefer not to work in schools with high minority populations (Orfield, Frankenberg and Lee, 2003).

High risk minority students are regularly saddled with ineffective teachers. (Nieto, 2003) If minority students are exposed to poor quality teachers as they are prepared for testing, is there any mystery in the negative results or the alleged achievement gap? When these children are ill-prepared for the test and are made to bear the consequences of bad teaching, this is unfair. This is a policy that discriminates.

Black and minority parents should not be misled by red herrings that are thrown out as examples of success in public education. Standardized testing is such a ruse. Testing is a political tool, not a demonstration of academic mastery. Anyone knows that if the same test is administered for more than five years, scores will increase. This does not mean that children are learning; it more than likely means that teachers understand how to better teach children to score higher on the test. The truth is no one clearly knows whether actual learning is taking place.

To aid political aims, the scoring formula in Florida has changed every year since the inception of the Florida Comprehensive Assessment Test (FCAT). I suspect this was done in order to manipulate the test results from year to year. FCAT is modeled after the Texas version. Ironically, both these states bear the recent imprimatur of the Bush oligarchy. In both cases, one cannot be sure that the eyes see what they see. For example, in Houston, Texas, Rod Paige's claims of success have been contravened by reports of inflated test scores and over exaggerated results, and high dropout rates.

Florida boasts improvement through 2004 but fails to mention increases in dropout rates and "options" for seniors who have reasonable grades but cannot pass the FCAT. Giving students a way out is another effort to prevent a public outcry whose political consequences may have ramifications. This is one example of a policy that is messaged to serve political rather than educational needs. Such discriminatory practices are not uncommon.

For example, it has been repeatedly demonstrated that black children are disproportionately represented in special education classes. Black children, due to racial bias, are ". . . three times more likely than their white counterparts to be labeled mentally retarded, forcing them into special education classes. . . ." (Matthews, 2001) This policy proceeds as a known quantity, but it goes quietly forward. According to Gene Carter of the Association for Supervision and Curriculum, "The oversimplification of students of color with special needs is a knee jerk response to a more complex problem." (Carter quoted in Matthews, 2001)

Even worse, these students are less likely than white children to be mainstreamed back into regular classes. This means that throughout their public education experience, they will be saddled with special needs labels, whether or not the proof of that label is ever verified in higher grades. Without any further assessment, the child is placed on track to receive a "special diploma." The result is that minority children are denied the opportunity of a quality education. (Matthews, 2001)

Finally, we must revisit here the issue of poverty as policy. Again, there are 34 million people in poverty in American; 13 million of those are children. (Relin, 2004) Poverty is an absolute enemy to public education because it never travels alone. It is not an excuse for failure. However, "It's estimated that about 40% of students in public schools need some kind of mental health care." (Vail, 2003) Additionally, many do not receive regular health care. (Vail, 2003) Poverty brings with it a host of problems -- not the least of which is that poor people do not get fair treatment, not even from the government.

I raise the question of poverty as a policy that discriminates because you cannot ignore it while trying to solve the problems of public education. The Carnegie Foundation has said that city schools, for example, cannot stress academic performance and turn a blind eye to the problems of poor children. (Vail, 2003) Poverty is not an excuse to fail but it can impact a child's ability to focus on learning.

Remember also that poverty controls where people live. Where they live, in turn, influences the kinds of schools that are available. We have demonstrated earlier that quality of education and quality of neighborhood exist as corollaries to one another. Here a question should be posed: if we know where the poor are concentrated, and if we know that poverty impacts education, why has there been no concerted effort outside education to counteract poverty and lift this segment of society?

For all the talk of reform and addressing the security needs of the nation, there is almost no talk of assaulting poverty. We worry about enemies being bred in impoverished countries a world away, but we ignore what festers within eyeshot of our planned communities. We are building affordable housing, hospitals and every sort of public accommodation in Iraq but ignoring blighted communities in America. Many America cities rival third world countries in their squalor.

The violence and anger that is brewing in these urban cauldrons will spill out and climb over the ivy covered walls of suburbia. Americans are going to have to begin looking further than their own front yards if they want to protect themselves. I have a vision problem. I can see pretty well at close range, but everything at a distance is blurry. America's vision is just the opposite. It seems to see everything at a distance, but that which is right at hand goes almost unnoticed.

The achievement gap is the result of the economic gap. Poverty changes the complexion of life possibilities for students as well as adults. The crucial problem is that those students who come to school needing more help tend not to get it. According to Jonathan Kozol, "The well-known facts are that school financing is vastly unequal and that students with wealthier parents are fortunate to live in towns that spend more on their education, whereas young people who live in financially strapped urban and rural areas are much less fortunate. (Kozol cited in Nieto, 2003) Kozol calls these differences "savage inequalities." The children who need the most help get the least. (Nieto, 2003) This kind of poverty is pernicious.

Poverty is neither hidden nor subtle. Sometimes it takes place within eyeshot of wealth. Schools, though not social agencies, find themselves in the position of having to address social needs because they have a direct impact on learning. (Vail, 2003) Vail says that "[t]he children in poverty's grip do not leave the miseries of their home lives behind them when they go to school." (Vail, 2003)

Schools are not always given the resources to deal with the various calamities that impact the lives of poor children. Many have to fend for themselves. Despite the lack of resources, some schools manage to open medical, dental and even mental health clinics in schools to combat the host of childhood ills that affect teaching and learning. (Vail, 2003) How can teachers deal with these issues when they are not trained to do so?

On the other hand, how can children learn when they are haunted by a sea of troubles they have not asked for but were born into? A child who lacks good nutrition and a stable home cannot learn as well as one who does. Hence, matters of education are influenced by matters of personal wealth – that is poverty or something else. When personal wealth fails, social wealth should intervene. However, selfishness in this area tends to take control.

For example, Florida is fighting its own version of a civil war. North Florida is controlled by white conservatives who look unfavorably on South Florida with its large Hispanic and black population. North Florida sought to flex its muscle in a 2004 Legislative Session by denying South Florida the District Cost Differential (DCD), a cost of living increase, which has been in place for years that adds millions of dollars to the education coffers of Miami-Dade and Broward counties. The DCD has been a part of the Florida Education Funding Program formula for years. South Florida has used these additional funds to combat the burden placed on the school system by the burgeoning immigrant population.

It is clear that the move to eliminate the DCD is the result of a few North Florida legislators who want to channel these funds into their own districts. Meanwhile, Miami-Dade County is estimated to lose approximately $18 million. This means that a school district that is 90% minority and that has 188 of its 340 schools receiving support from the federally funded Title I program for students on free and reduced lunch will lose a substantial portion of its budget.

While this may please North Floridians, it is the poor of Miami-Dade and Broward counties that will bear the brunt of this loss. This kind of policymaking piles a greater burden on a cash starved school district and an even greater loss of educational opportunity upon the poor. Miami is in the unenviable position of having to absorb the cost of a highly fluid immigrant population without always getting assistance from state and federal agencies.

This kind of policy demonstrates the insular and provincial nature of wealth and poverty. Miami, at one point, was named as one of America's poorest cities. That does not mean that everyone is poor, just that there is a high concentration of poverty. Certain pockets of Miami mirror the deprivation seen in cities like Mattapan, Massachusetts; East St. Louis, Missouri; or Oakland, California. Poverty is poverty. Hence, when school districts are robbed of resources for reasons that have nothing to do with children, this is tragic.

Another aspect of education that goes unnoticed is the high rate of suspensions and expulsions that put minority students out of school. Children come to school to get the skills they need to interact in society; yet, these policies tend to penalize students because they come to school without them. School officials, in response to much of the school related violence of high profile cases such as Columbine, Colorado in 1999 and subsequent cases, adopted zero tolerance policies that led to a host of bizarre suspensions and expulsions of students for carrying things as simple as finger nail clippers.

School officials began to mirror the politically driven actions of local police departments and courts which adopted *Three Strikes* and *Minimum Mandatory* sentencing guidelines that made garden variety, petty crimes worthy of the harshest penalties. Schools implemented a *Zero Tolerance* policy. Hence, there was a spike in the numbers of minority children displaced from schools. I am amazed at the number of students expelled from schools in my own district, a feature of the monthly Board meetings that goes almost unnoticed.

While I concede that there is not much room for error in the process of dealing with delinquent or potentially violent children, not nearly enough is being done to give minority children the benefit of the doubt because overcrowding does not give administrators the patience or luxury to try to reform children. In my own work with Neglected and Delinquent centers, talks with agencies trying to transition children back into schools are met by administrators who refuse to readmit these children – an illegal, if not immoral, act.

This shows a pattern of continuing to place the blame for adult failures on children. Children are not responsible for the conditions into which they are born. Minority children, saddled with the problems of racial prejudice and poverty, are doubly handicapped. So, when schools would rather suspend or expel minority students, they lose the best option, in many cases, for being able to move beyond the social limitations of their birth.

One of the critical problems is that teachers are hired to teach. They are generally not trained to deal with students who are unconventional. Certainly children are difficult, but most of them do not deserve to be abandoned before their 18th birthday. The public school system deals with this issue as they do most others; their mantra is, "we have neither the resources nor time." Many of these children are talented but without social skills. It is their inability to function within the social construct of schools that leads to their being discarded.

I suspect impatience with children is at the root of the plague of black and minority children being placed in special education classes at rates up to three times that of whites. Here's the rub: what does it say about our country when we become indifferent to children being discarded? Have we reached a point where our patience with children has brought us to think that they are disposable? Children deserve a better effort than that from adults.

When I think of poor children, I cannot help but think of the plight of street children throughout the world. In Mexico City, poor children wander the streets and spiral downward into crime, drug use and sexual exploitation. The children of Russia, Romania and the Philippines are at the mercy of sex tourists. Throughout the major cities of Brazil, poor children have become street urchins who fall victim to death squads and police-sanctioned murder. Is this what we want for the generations of children we refuse to teach? Surely, these children will end up somewhere. The McKinney-Vento Act attempts to buffer children against the more severe problems of homelessness by demanding that school district provide education and transportation services.

The rush to relieve American schools of the misery of dealing with difficult children will not absolve us of the debt society will pay. It is no coincidence that many of these children are minorities. Would we rather that they learn in schools or on the street? The cases are rare where the streets produce viable citizens.

Do I need to reiterate here that we cannot retreat into the provinces of walled-in comfort and expect trouble to stay outside our doors? Trouble knows no bounds. Education is still the best means to address many of the concerns mentioned here. Someone must be concerned about the fractionalization of America. Children and single mothers often bear the worst that society has to offer.

A few years ago, National Geographic reported that there are 27 million slaves in the modern world, many of these are children and women in war torn countries and were taken as prizes and discarded at will. Many Rwandan women who were victimized during the 1994 pogroms gave birth to children as the result of rapes and were infected with AIDS. In Sudan and Somalia, international aid organizations are trying to buy back women and children from their captors. In Thailand and India families sell their daughters for sex tourism. This is what happens to poor women and children worldwide when the affluent

When Americans see these things, they believe that they cannot go on inside America's borders. However, migrant networks exist in the United States where immigrant laborers are treated in the same fashion and held hostage. Within our own borders women are sold and traded as sex slaves. Florida, New York and California are havens of trafficking in human flesh. (Driscoll, 2004) We are not immune to the same problems we think of as unique to undeveloped countries. I raise these concerns because they are born out of indifference to the suffering of the less fortunate. They are also borne out of poor educational opportunities.

We have to question our own capacity for good when children become expendable and life becomes cheap. One need only walk into any inner-city school and see the fortified conditions or the disorder or the sheer uncleanness of the place to understand that we have not done our best. I have walked into schools and been moved to tears. If you are not moved, or if you only care about the "good" children, you miss the point of what education is supposed to do.

Marginalized populations within American culture get little sympathy. We can see this in the fact that we have people who are legally retarded on death row. We see this as we drive through major cities and never seem to notice the transition from clean to filthy or new to dilapidated in white neighborhoods versus inner-cities. We see indifference as people drive pass the homeless on their way to work, not taking the time to offer a prayer of support on their behalf. We see this when issues of discrimination against minorities is met with apathy in some cases and outrageous opposition in others.

Policies that discriminate affect all of us in the end. When the quality of life for anyone is diminished, the whole culture suffers. John Donne's *Meditation XVII* comes to mind where he said, "No man is an island entire of itself. Every man is a piece of the continent, a part of the main." Perhaps the true goal of America is not the acquisition of things but an unimpeachable sense of connectedness between its people.

The American ideology of self is a nationally destructive force. It is why we can see wealth and poverty, success and failure coexist in the same city. Discrimination is an insidious business. Whether for reasons of race or otherwise, policies that create vast differences in the learning opportunities for children undermine the fabric of the economy and weaken us even to the level of our neighborhoods.

Chapter Seven
Athletes, Entertainers and Academics

During the height of slavery, Africans brought from the continent would be dropped off at various points in the Caribbean, Central and South America and the Colonies of Great Britain (now the United States). Slaves, weary from the onerous journey of the Middle Passage and their long confinement in the holds of slave vessels, would be penned up and prepared for auction to the highest bidder. Neither the cries of mothers nor the shrieks of children were sufficient to deter the slave buyers from finding the best breeders or the strongest males.

Before the final auction, slaves were ordered to strip bare; their teeth were examined; and they were poked and prodded to make sure they were not defective. Slave traders became specialist in knowing how to identify good slaves versus bad ones? This wretched event was duplicated time and time again in various ports of call. This was about money. No one flinched at the inhumanity of it. It was for money. The slaves were at the mercy of their captors. They were property, not people. The traders sold flesh and reveled in their power. The slaves wondered where they would end up.

These days, a different kind of slave auction happens each year. Professional sports teams now place willing slaves, willing property -- if you will – up for auction and the meat market goes unnoticed as a neo-version of the old. To these auctions, the slaves come willingly. They even dress up and bring their lawyers, agents, mothers and fathers, if available. These slaves have been bred from youth to play with balls. They have been pampered and fed well. They believe themselves to be special. They have been told this from the beginning.

Prior to the auction, these slaves have undergone the same kinds of prodding and physical examination as their ancestors. They have been physically rated; this time by doctors. Their mental faculties are weighed via psychological tests; they run, leap and lift weights to show their endurance. Here, the slaves gladly show their physical gifts. *None of them are aware that this is an auction.*

So, the slaves are bought by billionaires, given work contracts and paid millions to become amusement for the public and to enhance the net worth of their beneficiaries. The interesting thing about this auction is that it has been transformed from the frightful experience of slaves crying out for their lost homeland and the deracination of their futures into a voluntary spectacle where people show up and cheer for the first slave picked. Here, the slaves want to make their masters rich. For this, black parents have turned their backs on the benefits of education in hopes that their children can be groomed into well-paid, willing slaves.

The trade-off for this new slavery is that you must do as you are told. You cannot criticize your master. You must perform on command. Most of all, you cannot speak up for black people in moments of crisis in America. Can you think of one athlete who spoke up for Rodney King, O. J. Simpson or James Byrd? *The best known athlete in the world – a basketball player at the time – made no public statement on race.*

For their silence, the slaves are rewarded handsomely and held up as paragons of the best blacks and minority people can become in America. This too is a ruse. However, back in the inner-cities of America, mothers and fathers look into the eyes of their children and wonder, "Are you the one or should we look for another?"

Athletes and entertainers have always been a source of cultural fascination. Today, their iconography has been transformed into a way of life. Hence, many parents have abandoned the notion of insisting that their children be successful in school; rather, on any given Saturday, they can be found in parks rather than libraries, encouraging their children to develop their physical skills while their brain surfaces remain smooth.

Companies such as Nike, Addidas and others hold summer camps for children as young as middle school. Promising athletes are given the means to relocate and attend schools where their talents can be further honed. While there are exceptions to every rule, most of these thoroughbreds are allowed to enter college with minimal ACT and SAT scores, given "scholarships" and groomed for another two or three years before they claim "hardship," a code word for "time to enter the draft," our modern-day slave auction.

The other area of modern enslavement is entertainment. Now, even white children want to be rappers. Minority children sit in class these days and write lyrics and ignore other lessons that are being taught. Rap is not new; it is poetry. Rap is no more innovative than Shakespeare. It is rhyme -- stressed and unstressed syllables and meter. Rap is literature set to music. Beatniks did it years ago in speakeasy clubs. Hence, throughout inner city areas makeshift studios are cranking out compact disks of poorly manufactured music where almost no one plays a musical instrument. This is the system that gives us our music moguls.

I received a call recently from a young man who wanted me to review a contract. He had left college and was now intent on pursuing a career in the music industry. I asked him what had happened with school. He had received a scholarship to play football. His reply was that he could not concentrate on school because his "mind was on his music." I had heard this too many times.

As I tried to explain the onerous contract he intended to sign no matter what I said, I could see he was under the influence of rap and marijuana. He was reeking. I tried to mitigate matters by telling him how important education was even if he was a success at music. I could see we was not about to be dissuaded. He had caught the entertainment bug.

Another aspect of entertainment has filtered into popular culture. Modest school attire has given in to urban wear. FUBU, Roca Wear, Phat Farm and others have made modest fortunes on the "wanna-be" nature of urban youth who have given up any hope of learning core subjects. Teachers are completely exasperated as young females continue to look more like ladies of the evening than students. So, like the slave auction, the educational impact has been that school is looked upon as a meaningless interruption to stardom.

Negative images are more damning to blacks than whites. The image of the comic, the clown, the savage athlete and the risqué woman are a death knell to all efforts to improve our position in America. The comic is a clown. The athlete is muscle, not mind. The semi-nude woman is property. This is why these images pervade American culture. Who takes the comic, the athlete or the dancing girl seriously?

This is possible because blacks and minority children are led to believe that owning a record label makes you a major player in the music industry. The real power in music is not the ability to make a record. People have been doing that in their garages for generations. The power in music rests in the hands of white-owned music companies that control the distribution of music worldwide. Without these powerbrokers, a recording might never be widely heard or distributed.

One need only remember Prince, the musician, who discovered this too late. His youthful enthusiasm for the music industry was greatly tempered when he realized that he was making the least from the music he created. So infuriated by his discovery was the mysterious musician that he changed his name to a "symbol" and wore the word "slave" on his cheek to protest the unfair practice of record companies taking the lion's share from unwitting musicians.

Most new musicians do not even take the time to realize that their first contract in the industry is nothing more than an onerous document where the record company makes millions and the artists make minimum. This was the reality that TLC, the Atlanta-based group, discovered when they ended their first series of national tours. By the time everyone got paid, they were in debt. Sadly, this lesson is repeated each year as new artists enter the industry.

P. Diddy, Russell Simmons, and Jay-Z notwithstanding, the music industry is a breeding ground for black exploitation. How quickly and successfully have we forgotten the slave market, the cries for freedom, the destruction of history, and the death of millions. Our past means nothing because we have been taught to only value the present. In fact, many believe that blacks have no past beyond America and Jamestown in 1619.

At the end of slavery and segregation, education was seen as a panacea for helping blacks and minorities to evolve in the American social milieu. Blacks rushed to enter any form of schooling available. Black colleges, generally started for the children of white slave masters, saw their ranks swell as blacks rushed to partake of higher education. Blacks fought for better schools, and fought to integrate white institutions.

Many of the athletes who attend predominantly white postsecondary schools as athletes are generally unaware of their schools' legacies of racial exclusion. Notable white coaching legends such as Paul "Bear" Bryant and others did not allow blacks on their teams until the inevitable shift of legal precedent and public pressure were brought to bear on their programs. Blacks proudly play on Saturdays for schools that have never apologized for their support of slavery, racism or segregation, never contributed a dollar toward reparations and never acknowledged their collusion in the nationwide conspiracy to destroy black people.

Athletes have forsaken any questioning of their schools' histories in favor of the farm system that propels them toward wealth and stardom despite the fact that most of these programs graduate fewer than 40% of their black athletes with college degrees. In fact, Georgia Tech and Connecticut, the two NCAA Men's Basketball finalists, respectively, only graduated 27% of their players with college degrees over a six year period. "Of the 65 teams in the [2004 men's] tournament,

44 fell below the 50% graduation rate that a group of sports reformers has proposed as a minimum standard for participation in post-season play. The graduation rate was below 20% for 10 teams, and zero for four." (Basketball's Academic Fouls, 2004)

Yet, the coaches of these teams are idolized for having character and for caring about their charges. Many of the young men, on the other hand, are not aware of the need to grasp the golden ring of education because their chances of reaching the professional level are limited. Without a proper education, they are left to flounder in failure and obscurity.

The education of minority children has been severely crippled by this process. Athletes and entertainers have replaced educated professionals as role models for minority children. When a room full of minority children are asked about their career choices, almost invariably several boys will declare they intend to become athletes. The athlete and the entertainer are the same; they work for the amusement of others.

I have no problem with any person who follows the gift that God has given him. I am reminded here of the prophet Jeremiah's admonition from God about his abilities. While questioning himself, Jeremiah is told "Before I formed thee in the belly, I knew thee; and before thou camest forth out of the womb, I sanctified thee, and I ordained thee a prophet unto the nations." (Bible, KJV,

Jeremiah 1:5) They are called to be athletes just as others are ordained to be artists. Would anyone believe otherwise of Serena Williams or Alex Rodriguez? So, I have no trouble with Tiger Woods, Lebron James, Michael Jordans, or Jay-Z. They were meant to be from the beginning. I wish them power.

My concern is for the would-be stars who have abandoned education. I am concerned about the students who leave school without a diploma. Moreover, I am adamantly against our present educational system that continues to reinforce failure and then makes the children suffer by not allowing them to graduate after they have been only minimally prepared for life after high school. Also, I am against the valuation of Lebron James over Dr. Ben Carson. Which is more valuable to you: a basketball player or a neurosurgeon? In the end, what will it matter if basketball succeeds or fails?

Black and minority children are being sold the idea that education is no longer the way for them to succeed. They are being sold the premise that athletics and entertainment are the domain of the many rather than the few. *Here's the news: the majority of minority children are going to have to work in traditional positions for a living!* Education is still the primary means by which most children – minority or otherwise – are going to succeed in life. Stardom is an exception, not a rule.

The proof is in the stark reality that very few athletes make it to the professional level. There are only about 5,000 such jobs available in the first place. The NCAA conducted a study of the chances for athletes to make it from college to the professional ranks and reported the following:

NCAA	# of high School Students	% college students to Professional Ranks	Average Career**
Men's Basketball	1,540,597	1 in 5,300	4-6 years
Football	1,023, 712	1 in 9,300	4-5 years
Baseball	451,674	1 in 1,500	4-7 years

*The NCAA News, November 6, 2002.
**Sage, 1990

Here is the stark reality of placing one's hope in a sports career. Professional basketball and football have the two worst records of yielding a successful result for would-be players. It is evident from these numbers that only the extraordinarily gifted will make it beyond college.

When one looks at the likes of Michael Jordan, Lisa Leslie, Kobe Bryant, Allen Iverson, Clinton Portis, Peyton Manning, there is only one thing you can conclude. These folk were gifted beyond measure in their respective sports. "Overall only about 5 percent of high school athletes . . . play at the collegiate level, 3 percent play at the professional level, and two-tenths of 1 percent make it to the professional sport level." (Sage, 1990) They represent that elite level of athleticism that most of us can only dream about. Rational people, at some point, realize that life holds another path for them.

Moreover, the control of major sports is still in the hands of white males. This very elite group is invariably among the wealthiest Americans according to the Forbes list of America's most affluent citizens. "Control of sports is unequally distributed among social classes, and in fact almost totally resides in the wealthy and powerful social groups. Owners of professional sports teams are among the wealthiest people in the United States. Each year the richest 400 people in America are identified and profiled in *Forbes* magazine; invariably, 20 to 30 of them are professional sports team owners." (Sage, 1990) Sage goes on in his monumental work to indicate that sports reflect society's prejudices; and they do not provide a panacea to the inequities of American society in general.

Unfortunately, black and minority children fill playgrounds and ignore libraries. Their imaginations are replete with images of black athletes driving sports cars, living in exorbitant homes and garnering all kinds of public attention. They are also enamored with the thought of moving up in social class. But the truth of the matter is that sports represent a very narrow window of opportunity for a very small coterie of gifted athletes. "[T]he potential for sports to directly provide social mobility for significant numbers of Americans in largely imaginary." (Sage, 1990)

It is this ephemeral quality that renders the sports dream so out of reach for most minorities. My problem is that not just the children, but parents are now buying into this notion of the child-athlete. It has gotten to the point that trying to reason with both children and parents has reached a critical mass. Reason must prevail. Reason tells us that our children have a better chance if they invest their energies in school rather than sports.

Another point of contention here is the influence of the sports and entertainment culture upon minority children. America is stratified by race and class. The privileged few who make it in sports have begun to make their private lives public. Television shows such as *Cribs*.

While I never watch such shows, I happened to see in passing one rapper who spoke about the $25,000 bed spread he had purchased. While I understood his pride, I could not help but think of how this sum could have funded the college education of some minority student – at least to a degree. Which is more valuable: a student or a spread? These kinds of exhibitions show that money does not give the possessor class.

Education is in no position to compete with sports or entertainment. I've almost gotten to the point that I no longer accept invitations to school career days. The only thing the students want to know is how much money I make. Professionals and college graduates are not looked at as successful. Children do not view black professionals as viable role models.

Robert Johnson is now the majority owner of the Charlotte Bobcats, the former Hornets NBA franchise. Johnson, now a billionaire after his sale of BET, is a majority shareholder, not a sole owner. (Patel and Cronin, 2003) He is the first black majority owner of a major sports team. He has recently been joined in the ranks of ownership by rapper Jay-Z. This is one of the few positive trends in sports. But it is not the business side that attracts our youth. There have been no black majority owners of major franchises prior to Johnson because ownership is the province of billionaires. (Patel and Cronin, 2003) By the way, Johnson was the only black person to make it to the Forbes list of America's 400 wealthiest people.

Again, I ask the question: what has happened to our hunger for education? Can times be more desperate for black people? Recently, *The Miami Herald* published a series of articles called "Justice Withheld" which demonstrated that blacks are most likely to receive their worst treatment in America at the hands of the criminal justice system. This prompted Leonard Pitts, a recent winner of the 2004 Pulitzer Prize for journalism to write an open letter to African-America men that pleaded the following: *"Could you please stop being such good customers of the American justice system. I am sick to my soul of watching shaggy-haired black boys and men in orange jumpsuits led into courtrooms to*

*be judged for doing some stupid and heinous thing.
I'm weary of the old Richard Prior line about how
he went to court looking for justices and that's what
he found. 'Just us.'"* (Pitts, 2004)

Yet, the image of the gangster and thug has become common. Boys, girls, men and women want to be notorious rather than of sound reputation. I've seen more underwear in the last few years in public than I care to remember. Most minority children don't even know that the style came from prison where inmates are not allowed to wear belts. It is this diffusion of negative imagery into the wider culture that troubles me. This is no accident. The makers of fashion are only concerned about dollars, not about children.

While white children have the luxury of experimenting with fads, black and Hispanic children are viewed with suspicion from the outset. They are followed in stores, presumed thieves, arrested and ticketed at higher rates than whites and convicted more often. Much of this comes from misperceptions about their character and is based on stereotypes portrayed in the media and music. Then strangely, blacks embrace all that is negative up to and including the use of the word *nigger* as standard conversation?

When I walk into school buildings these days, the vestiges of racism are everywhere. During a recent visit to Philadelphia, I visited a large middle school. I knew before I entered the building what it would be like. I have come to know that if the exterior is terrible, what goes on inside the building is very likely to be terrible as well. That's not always the case; but more often than not, it is true. Upon entering this Philadelphia school through the cafeteria, I found black children wearing the garb of urban America. As I walked through the building, the noise level did not bespeak a good learning environment.

By the time I finished a conversation with a mathematics instructor, I was convinced that this place was not doing a good job of educating children. This school had the committed teachers who were just overwhelmed by the totality of working with children who had no concept of order. This experience came on the heels of my reading an article that 1/2 of the teachers in Philadelphia's public schools who had taken the state competency test had failed. Children could not be blamed for that. (Khetan, 2004)

Philadelphia mirrors most major American cities. The whites have fled to the suburbs, built new schools that are 80% or more white, depleted the tax base, and left public schools for minorities and lower middle class whites to fester in. Still, what I saw in this school was not the fault of whites. It was the fault of administrators who had lost hope in the face of problems they do not have the strength to confront. Black and minority children are caught in a nearly inescapable web of mediocrity. The teachers in these schools have been left to fend for themselves. At the same time, many students have abandoned hope of learning core subjects. But there are reasons to be encouraged.

Education cannot be abandoned. We have struggled too hard to achieve the privilege of having public education. What is the logic of foregoing education for the possibility of a career in sports or entertainment that is almost unattainable? This attraction to fame is another ruse that blacks and minorities tend to follow. When we take pursuit of these illusory careers, we tend to lose focus on the urgency of learning.

Two of my heroes are Dr. Benjamin Carson and Reginald Lewis. Carson, a world renowned neurosurgeon grew up in Baltimore's roughest neighborhood, but he accepted the challenge of education. After the usual stint of academic disinterest, Carson realized that good grades brought positive attention his way. He was a most unassuming person but took on the challenge of a career in neurosurgery because he was repeatedly told that blacks could not succeed there. To date, he has performed some of the most complex operations involving the separation of conjoined twins and the removal of half the brain to prevent seizures. Yet, his name is seldom mentioned when blacks speak of success.

Reginald, Lewis, an irrepressible investment banker, leveraged the purchase of the Beatrice Corporation in 1987. Lewis was inexhaustible and energetic and refused to allow himself to be held within any limits concocted on the basis of color. He bought Beatrice International Foods for $985 billion through a combination of business savvy and financial creativity. My most salient memory from his biography was how he talked his way into Harvard's Law School after playing football at Virginia State College. Lewis always thought he would be a success. He and Carson were polar opposites, but each represented the good things that can come from graduate and professional careers.

We live in an age when athletes, even the worst of them, make exorbitant sums. To be frank, it is difficult to get children to see the logic of college and graduate or professional school when the average salary in the NBA is $4 million; the average for MLB is $1.9 million; and the average for the NFL is $1.1 million. (Hughes, 2003) Nor does it help that Lebron James made $90 million before his first NBA game. But they must be properly apprised of the folly of this venture.

There is a madness at work here that must be confronted. The distortion of present American society is that we place our value on the unimportant. We also fail to recognize the long term effects of present decisions. What message are we giving to children that sports figures make more than teachers? Children are perceptive. They have enough acumen to understand that the risk of being successful in music and athletics is worth taking. What they don't realize is that the chances for success are not in their favor.

That gamble is like going to Las Vegas. The Strip cannot stay open unless it takes in more money than it gives away – much more money. It is rigged in favor of the casinos. Likewise, success in sports and entertainment is rigged in favor of the powerbrokers. Remember, owners must approve other owners in major league sports. This reminds me of restrictive covenants with rights of first refusal. Robert Johnson, Magic Johnson, Michael Jordan and Jay-Z notwithstanding, team ownership is still primarily the domain of wealthy white men.

I happened to be in Washington, D.C. at the time Michael Jordan retired from the Washington Wizards. He had altruistically played for two seasons on worn out knees and given the Wizards some of their most exciting games. As part owner of the team, he had exerted some pressure on his teammates to get better, but it did not work out. When his second season ended, the majority owner of the team summoned Jordan to his office and summarily dismissed him from the ownership group. For all his appeal, Jordan discovered that he was a millionaire in a billionaire's world.

What does race have to do with athletics and entertainment? Simple: amusement. Sports and entertainment are meant to take the mind off reality. The word *amuse* (not to think) is the opposite of *muse* (which means to think intently). Blacks want to major in amusement. Perhaps this is a defense mechanism; but amusement is really a tool for white Americans. They want to forget the injustices that exist; and by paying a few of us to amuse millions, the hope is that we'll forget that our streets are unsafe. I, for one, am not amused at black children who don't know that rapping and academic success take exactly the same skill – repetition.

Is there no balance or middle ground? Yes, we must begin to help children know the difference between the possible and the impossible. This does not mean that we rob them of their ability to dream. Were it not for dreaming, how could I – a product of Overtown – go to law school at the University of Miami? What I mean here is that skill sets must be recognized and properly directed. The majority of our children need to understand that education provides a viable chance. Everything in life is chance. But take the best one!

I recognized early on that I was no athlete. By high school, it was clear that I was stuck at five-foot six inches. I was fair at sports, but I bore no resemblance to my idols Dr. J or Tony Dorsett. I did know that I was good with words. I loved books from the start. My father had gone to the third grade, but he loved to read. He read everything he could get his hands on. I wanted to be like him. So, I read constantly.

By the time I graduated from high school, I was number five in my class. I received a full scholarship to Morehouse College in Atlanta, Georgia. I later received a full scholarship to Atlanta University. Then, I later received a full scholarship to the University of Miami School of

Law. I attended college for nine consecutive years on scholarships. This all happened because I chose education. I did not have to do this, but it was the best option for me. I never won a Heisman, but I did become a *Phi Beta Kappa,* the highest academic honor one can receive as an undergraduate. The point here is that I realized my path, and I was supported in that pursuit by teachers who saw more in me than I saw in myself. To this day, I still visit teachers from elementary school through college to thank them for helping me to see my way.

Life has not always been good. I used to hide in the store to keep my classmates from seeing me buy things with food stamps. I've gone to school hungry and with no lunch money. I've eaten cereal with corn syrup for sugar. When it rained, it rained as much indoors as outside, and we placed pots on the floor to catch water. I can still remember the damp feeling in the house days after the rain had stopped. I've also killed more than a few large roaches in my day. I've known poverty. So, when I hear these claims of hardship, I know a little something about that.

Finally, I knew that my success would mean something for generations. I was the first in my family to complete college, the first to earn a graduate degree, and the first to have a professional career. Now, as my nieces and nephews are making their way into college, I see that the sacrifice was not in vain. I want the athlete to be the athlete. I want the entertainer to be the entertainer. I want the scholar to be the scholar. I want parents to know the difference.

Chapter Eight
Public Education as Preparation for Prison

Public schools serve the needs of prisons, one of America's fastest growing industries. Like Wal-Mart, prisons are becoming major employers in rural and urban centers. America, allegedly the most industrialized nation in the First World, warehouses nearly 2 million of its citizens – some deservedly so – in prisons more elaborate and expensive than any high school. The figure does not include the hundreds of children mired in juvenile justice systems across the country. What does it mean when America spends approximately $8,000 annually to educate a child and $20,000 annually to incarcerate inmates? We spend more on people we have thrown away than on children we who we claim to cherish.

Yet, prison is the holding place for many poorly, educated citizens; and, for minorities, prison is almost an expected life experience. The *Christian Science Monitor* reported in 2003 that "if current trends continue, it means that a black male in the United States would have about a 1 in 3 chance of going to prison in his lifetime. For a Hispanic male, it's 1in 6; for a white male, 1 in 17." (Chaddock, 2003)

Using the position that prisoners represent cheaply exploited labor source, "about 3.5% of the 2.1 million prisoners in the USA produced goods and services worth an estimated $1.5 billion in

2002." (Swartz, 2004) About twelve states have call centers in state and federal prisons, and other industries using prisoner services include or have included Dell Computers, Departments of Motor Vehicles, Delco-Remy (car parts); some 2,000 inmates work as call center representatives nationwide. (Swartz, 2004) Swartz says in his article that "As prison populations swell, so has the number of potential qualified workers." Pay for an inmate averages about $200 per month. (Swartz, 2004)

When a child does not receive quality training for a career or college, he or she is at the mercy of capitalism. Everything in America glorifies wealth as a way of life, but minority children are saddled with a parallel existence that puts them in the position of Tantalus, able to see the fruit but never to taste it. Poverty and wealth are familiar with one another but sworn enemies. Poverty fights to keep its victims. Real wealth struggles to keep the poor and the *nouveau riche* at bay.

Poverty is the enemy of education and the friend of prisons. An inordinately high number of prisoners are also poorly educated. According to Bureau of Justice Statistics, 68% of the prison population did not receive a high school diploma. (U.S. Department of Justice, 2004) As state assessments render more and more minority students unable to access the workplace, they increase their chances of becoming customers of America's prisons.

Prison and poor education are a boon for the prison industry. For example, according to Christian Parenti, Pelican Bay Prison is the largest employer in California's Del Norte County. (Parenti, 1999) Large prisons are moving into economically depressed and rural areas with the promise of jobs, an irresistible lure for local politicians desperate to stimulate their economies and create jobs. Large cities are using these prisons as dumping grounds for all manner of offenders and those prisoners represent an inexhaustible labor supply with no voting rights.

In Pendleton, Oregon, they have managed to turn prisoners into profit. They manufacture a brand of jeans called *Prison Blues*. These oversized baggy jeans are on sale online from the penitentiary. Just think about it. The company can make jeans using prison labor for less than minimum wage. Why use child labor in a Third World country when you can use people with no voting voice in the United States. My first reaction to *Prison Blues* was horror; then, I realized that this is what corporations do. They take advantage of opportunities. Prisoners have minimal skills; they don't have unions and need no health insurance. Hence, they are modern day slaves -- no pay or little pay required.

As with all things, there is no fairness in the criminal justice system. In early 2004, the *Miami*

Herald published a scathing report on racism in the criminal justice system by demonstrating that blacks and whites get distinctly different penalties for the same crimes. More often than not whites had their adjudications withheld, resulting in no criminal record while blacks were usually sentenced to jail time. (Garcia and Grotto, 2004)

The article states that "[w]hite criminal defendants in Florida are nearly 50 percent more likely than blacks to get a withhold of adjudication, a plea deal that blocks their felony convictions even when they plead to the crime. White Hispanics are 31% more likely than blacks to get a withhold." (Garcia and Grotto, 2004) After examining more than 800,000 cases from 1993-2002, the *Miami Herald* found ". . . a system that is more likely to punish blacks than whites in the same predicament." (Garcia and Grotto) This was not news to black people. The article was so compelling that it led Leonard Pitts, another Herald columnist, to plead with blacks to stay out of the clutches of the criminal justice system. In case after case, blacks and whites charged with the same crimes received different results.

The question here is: what hope does a black child have when he is confronted with recognizing that the criminal justice system means him no good? Of course, this is after he has been rejected by an educational system that made him feel irrelevant. During each board meeting in Miami-Dade County, as is the case across the country, children are expelled from school. These children are thrown into a position to be swallowed up by the penal system. With no skills and no resources, they are at the mercy of system after system.

Every time I hear of the death of a young male at the hands of the police, I try to follow the education trail. Invariably, you will find that very few college going young men, black or white, are killed by the police. Miami's race riots have been sparked time and again over policeman killing black males. When I hear of these atrocities, I am reminded of the clear correlation between crime and low levels of education. Remember we indicated earlier in this chapter that 68% of prisoners, according to the Department of Justice, do not have high school diplomas.

Need I note here that the *Herald* article raised no real stir in Miami? The article demonstrated racial preference. Seldom do whites oppose this type of affirmative action. It demonstrates that we do no have the political will to confront real problems. In his book *The Debt (2001)*, Randall Robinson says we see racial problems but lack the will to address them. Miami, in true American fashion, allowed the flame to shine on racism, flicker for a moment and then go out.

There was no criminal investigation. Who would you indict? The judges see it. The prosecutors know it. The public defenders and criminal defense attorneys are aware. Yet, the article made only a ripple in the community. The point is that black victims are not worth righteous indignation that cuts across racial or ethnic lines.

This, by the way, is not a black problem. blacks and Hispanics are the two largest subgroups in prison. The Department of Justice 2001 summary of the prison population showed that blacks represented 46% of the nearly 2 million persons in prison with sentences of more than one year. (Harrison and Beck, 2001) At the same time blacks are 12% of the national population. In state after state, blacks are two to three times more likely than their white peers to be incarcerated. If the *Herald* article's premise can be extrapolated, then the problem is national, widespread and tragic. It is a problem that deserves the attention of our best minds.

What's worse are the problems that incarceration creates after the sentence has been served. A convicted felony cannot own a gun, vote or hold certain jobs. Life possibilities are severely limited. My principle problem here is the loss of the right to vote. This silences the voices of millions both in prison and millions who have served their sentences. Many young people who become involved in crime at an early age cannot fathom the long-term effect such a loss of privilege has on their lives. Even worse, there is no legally justifiable reason why this negation of voting privilege persists. So, when education belches forth its rejects and prison embraces them, the consequence can be lifelong isolation.

Fifty years after *Brown,* here we are staring a new reality in the face, the wholesale incarceration of millions of our most undereducated citizens without taking a look at the factors that got them there. We tend to see the end result, the criminal, and miss the process that creates the criminal. Americans are afraid of children, and the children are becoming more aggressive. Their aggressiveness is in part exploration on societal limits. Without adult guidance to provide cutoff points, children become criminals. That's disgraceful.

I remember reading a book years ago called *A Clockwork Orange* by Anthony Burgess. A quintessential question of the book was whether the main character Alex, a seemingly incorrigible young man, prone to criminal behavior, was born evil or was he the product of a society that made him evil. Alex was the key figure in a culture run amuck with children making adults cower in fear. More and more, we are beginning to bear the marks of that book.

When black and minority children are victimized in poor educational environments, are they at fault? When black students enter school, only 20% of them have the basics of reading to be considered ready to learn (*USA Today*, April 29, 2004) The "average black student who graduates from high school is equipped with the skills the average white student mastered by eighth grade . . . ." (*USA Today*, April 29, 2004) This is the result of being exposed to schools where as many as 50% of their teachers are not degreed or certified in the subjects they teach. (*USA Today*, April 29, 2004)

These same children are being labeled as failures as early as third grade. Later, that same child is asked to take a test to earn a diploma. What I see here is a system that reinforces early on and repeatedly that these students have little chance of succeeding. Who needs slavery when education does a more effective job?

The education system and the criminal justice system exist in a strange symbiosis. We know very early on which children are moving back and forth between the two. In Miami, we have at least two full-blown schools housed in detention facilities, one with as many as two hundred students. One must laude the people who work in these places for their courage at trying to salvage children that society and parents have, in some cases, given up for lost. When I walk into these buildings, my own mental faculties are traumatized by the solemnity of the surroundings. Barbed wire, heavy metal doors and prison attire are merged with language arts and mathematics lessons. When I look at the students I wonder how they can maintain any level of civility in these places. That they do hold it together is a testament to their skillful, loving teachers. Susan Castleman and Beverly Childs, two teachers in Miami who willingly work with this student population, deserve the highest praise.

Allow me for a moment here to digress into the problem of the glorification of criminal life. Education is as much formal as informal. Today's children are exposed to an informal education through mass media and music that glorifies pimps, pole dancers and illicit behavior. The height of insult in this regard in recent months was David Chang's attempt to market a game called *Ghettopoly.* This game involves drinking 40s (malt liquor), pimping women and drugs. I was appalled that Chang, himself Asian, could not see the inherent insult in the matter. However, how am I to scold Chang and leave Nelly, a rapper, unscathed for his promotion of a drink called Pimp Juice? These are examples of the informal mis-education of minority children and the lauding of socially unacceptable behavior. Other rappers can be seen in videos using a woman's hind parts to swipe a credit card.

As our children are turning away from public education, here is a chasm of iniquity waiting to embrace them. While for the stars this is all an act, poorly educated black children are embracing this as real life drama. Even what has become fashionable in urban wear -- showing one's underwear by letting one's pants ride low – is a style stolen from prisoners who are not allowed to wear belts in prison and must wear whatever size is available.

Again, this is not a black or minority problem. The music industry's real power is still in the hands of major record labels. They hold the power to distribute and get air play for records that are produced by artists all over the country. These images are mass produced and mass distributed through compact discs and MTV to audiences worldwide. At the same time children are failing school, they are majoring in the unethical. The low road has become mainstream. Again, whose problem is it anyway? We tend to be what my mother called "two-faced" about what we expect. You cannot tell children to have standards and then use the most powerful means at your disposal to perpetuate the lowering of those standards.

Here is my two cents worth on prison and education. Prison is a given. If you don't prepare yourself for something good as a black or minority person in America, you increase your chances for incarceration. Education isn't for everyone. Bill Gates' unbounded success proves that. However, minority children come into the world fighting a host of setbacks, racism, discrimination, poverty stereotypes, historical omissions of their contributions to the success of this country, and presumptions against their intelligence. Therefore, minority children do not have the luxury of failing to do their best.

In the case of blacks, when you lead in all the negative categories of life (e.g., lowest life expectancy, highest death rate, high dropout rates, and lowest average income), these are good incentives to take full advantage of a free public education. No one feels sorry for the plight of minority children – save a few honest folk who acknowledge that the children's circumstances are not deserved. Hence, there must be a hunger and thirst for education and a desire to advance in life that is commensurate with the opportunity given.

Prison should not be an option. Too often among young minority children, there is a feeling that a stint in jail is a badge of honor. However, in working with children who really want a way out, I find that what they really want is firm adult leadership in their lives. I sat in a meeting a few days ago while a young man who is temporarily housed at the Miami Bridge, a crisis agency for school-aged children, praised the structured life he had in the shelter. Conversely, he begged not to go back to his public high school, my alma mater, because his grades in the shelter were so much better. He beamed with pride over making "A's" and "B's."

While I was excited for him, I learned several things. First, children want structure, not friendship from adults. Children naturally rebel against authority, but if properly administered, they come to understand that it is in their best interest. This young man was thriving because his day was completely structured from beginning to finish. This is what schools and parents need to adopt. Children cannot be left to the haphazard life of rearing themselves. They need guidance. Second, I learned that children – even those who are deemed unmanageable – welcome continuity when it leads to identifiable achievement. This young man shunned a regular school campus because he could see results from the direction he was receiving at the Miami Bridge. Third, school is a much better alternative than jail. Without intervention, this young man was a prime candidate for jail. Yet, he yielded to sound guidance, rigid structure and trustworthy adult leadership.

If we are to educate children and keep them out of jail, it dawned on me that we must have a new education model in inner-city schools. The Miami Bridge, under the leadership of Stephanie Solovei, an irrepressible child advocate, has gained a reputation for intervention with children because it practices sound child intervention strategies. Schools are going to have to learn more from these groups.

When the young man mentioned above told his story and refused to return to my high school, I recalled the disorder that reigned there during my last visit. While high schools are active places, a school with two consecutive "F" grades on the state assessment clearly needs more structure. The Miami Bridge has a formula for education that works.

First, the teacher is certified and committed. All too often, inner-city schools are dumping grounds for the newest, the least certified and the least motivated teachers. Susan Castleman, the teacher at the Miami Bridge, loves children and chose this population to work with. She labors with these children. Knowing she may only have them for a maximum of thirty days, she gives no excuses and she gives no quarter.

Second, the Bridge has a small classroom concept. Factory-style schools are the province of poor children. The children of suburbia are not exposed to schools that dehumanize them in noisy, disorderly environments. Even teenagers are still adjusting socially. Not every one of them can function in a large school. Public schools need to adopt smaller School Within a School models.

At-risk students cannot get the attention they deserve in overcrowded classrooms. The young man from the Miami Bridge spoke about how much "getting attention" meant to him. I saw in this a simple solution to a chronic problem. Children who do not get enough attention tend to cause trouble; that is their way of demanding attention.

Third, the Miami Bridge thrives on high expectations for its charges. From the moment children enter the Miami Bridge, there is a system of rewards built in their daily schedule for doing the right thing. How often is good work rewarded? These points lead to the ability to purchase small necessities and niceties not normally available to the student from an in-house store. These points also lead to trips to college and professional sporting events. The children know their parameters; therefore, they can figure out how to function. We tend to believe that children in public education learn these things as they matriculate. Many do, but many do not. Hence, the clear communication and reinforcement of expectations give the children the support they need to be successful.

Another successful program can be found at COPE Center South in Miami, a school for pregnant girls. Dr. Sandra Billingslea oversees a program there called the *Building Eager Esteem (BEE) Club*. Being a master motivator, Dr. Billinglsea takes girls who have made wrong choices early and rebuilds their self-esteem to a point where her students are able to return to their home schools, graduate and attend college. Extraordinary teachers are the perfect antidote to the possibility of incarceration. Dr. Billingslea is a Point of Light in her community. She goes wherever she has to go to get children on the right track. This is a model worth duplicating.

One final word on prison: the only solution is not to go there. We must actively work to keep minority children out of the clutches of the criminal justice system by expanding what we do in education. Teacher training will need to include, as a regular feature, how to deal with aggressive and hard to manage children. Presently, teachers receive instruction in classroom management based upon a view of education that is outmoded.

Teachers must learn to deal with children who are dealing with parents dying of AIDS, extreme poverty, psychological fragility and a general feeling of being unsafe. We ask a great deal of teachers already, but this one thing must be added. Again, I say train teachers but pay them better. How much is a Susan Castleman or Dr. Sandra Billingslea worth?

Chapter Nine
Build It and They Will Come

For minorities, the answer to the public schools crisis is to build the kind of schools that teach the kind of values they appreciate. *Minorities place all their hope in a public school system that was not designed for them.* Issues such as teacher distribution, historically distorted curriculum, and a condescending view of minority children are standards of public education. (Hilliard, 1999)

Minority parents should remember the evolution of public education in America. It was not designed for everyone. Education began in America as a mirror of European models. That is, education was reserved for the elite, then for white males. It did not initially include women, minorities and blacks especially. Education was inextricably connected to power; therefore, its acquisition was seen as the province of a few – that is, powerful men.

The original purpose of education in America was moral and religious education. The Massachusetts Acts of 1642 and the Old Deluder Satan Act of 1647 were the foundation of support for compulsory public education. Hence, the Puritan church was a leader in public education and in the fight to bring public education to former slaves and Native Americans. One of the earliest schools for blacks was started by Elias Neau in 1704 in New

York City. However, generally whites did not support the education of blacks initially.

The thought of establishing private schools should not frighten black people. ". . . African people brought thousands of years of excellence traditions with them, struggled mightily to preserve those systems during enslavement, and ultimately, upon emancipation, they established immediately more than 500 independent schools." (Hilliard, 2002) Therefore, we should not have to rustle up the courage. If former slaves could do it, we have no excuses.

Education prior to *Brown* was separate and unequal. It was unequal because blacks and minorities were not intended to catch up with their oppressors. This lasted long past 1954. Many of the colleges that became the training ground for black teachers and ministers were originally established by the churches and white philanthropists who saw the need for the 4 million freed slaves to life themselves through education. However, access to quality public education remained elusive for blacks. Some schools never desegregated and certain schools and school districts remain separate and unequal to date.

Events such as the Cold War and the space race heightened the need for more professionals. Yet, blacks remained isolated in their quest for equity in education. Black teachers had to fight to get pay equal to that of white teachers. (Dunn, 1997) During the days of segregation, one teacher at Booker T. Washington High School in Miami was run out of town for seeking equal pay for blacks. (Dunn, 1997)

Blacks received meager support for their schools, and materials were usually passed down from white schools, if at all. Resources were often withheld intentionally. The objective was simple. Black and minority children were not meant to be given the skills to compete with whites. This was true then; and, judging from the disparate quality of education the two groups receive today, the same holds true today. According to John Logan (2002), "Separate means unequal in American public education." The average 12th grade student of color reads at the level of an 8th grader. (Nieto, 2003)

One common denominator to pre-Brown and post-Brown is that whites have always had their private schools. These schools were designed to train the nation's leaders and to protect the values of the aristocracy. Students from these schools were expected to matriculate at Ivy League universities and move into positions of power in business and government. Many of these schools still serve the same purpose today. Their traditions are about excellence and access to power. The new, upper middle class version of this is the neighborhood charter school. These schools are designed to duplicate the values of white hegemony.

The public education system in America is not designed for the advancement of minorities or the poor. They are designed for the "average"

American, who is neither black, minority nor poor. These institutions are corrupt in that they are designed to defeat the hopes of minority people. For example, it is no coincidence that blacks are 12% of the national population and 46% of the people in prison. From state to state, blacks are in prison at a rate two to three times their presence in the general population.

The other reasonable conclusion is that the criminal justice system is doing exactly what it is designed to do, eliminate blacks from the general population. I remind you here of the *Miami Herald* article discussed earlier. Do you really believe judges and lawyers did not see that blacks were receiving a raw deal before the *Herald* reported that whites were being favored? I noticed it within days. Yet, there is abject silence and a complete lack of outrage that the criminal justice system is an enemy to the black community – especially to black males, black attorneys and officers notwithstanding.

We should never underestimate the destructive power of racism or its imprint on the psyche of black Americans. This is not a victim's mentality. When the notion of feeling victimized is raised about blacks, one should take note that this too is a red herring, a thought thrown into the public discourse to distract attention from the real problem – racism. "This age-old strategy of scapegoating the most vulnerable, frightening the most insecure, and supporting the most comfortable constitutes a kind of iron law signaling the decline of modern civilizations . . . ." (West and Gates, 1996) The overrepresentation of blacks in prison is a factual observation, not a biased or emotional one.

I remind you here that during the height of his struggle with AIDS, the late tennis star Arthur Ashe indicated that race, not AIDS, was his greatest burden in life. (Ashe quoted in Tatum, 1997) If I had to weigh Ashe's opinion of race versus that of Shelby Steele's, I would side with Ashe. Ashe's comment demonstrates that privilege does not dull the piercing effects of color-based prejudice. His comments also indicate that the albatross of racism hanging about the neck of a black person for life is more threatening than impending death.

Decisions in all aspects of American life are impacted by race. Just as race impacts criminal justice, politics, religion and housing, it is present and prevalent in public education. "It is a real pity that even at this moment, the majority view in virtually all surveys of education indicate the belief that some races are simply more intelligent than others." (Hilliard, 1999) We would like to believe that education is exempt for racial profiling but the existence of a wealth of literature alleging the inferiority of dark skin peoples (e.g., *The Bell Curve*) remain popular reading and are considered staples in the teaching academy.

One need only look at the schools in minority neighborhoods versus those in white neighborhoods to verify the obvious. Public education has no proven track record to demonstrate that its intentions toward blacks are good. Hence, blacks and Hispanics must work together to act affirmatively to build their own schools, not abandoning the public school system, but to provide viable, competitive alternatives.

I should like to deal here with the question of the Latino presence in public education. Latinos have had their own battles for equity. In 1945, a class action suit was filed on behalf of five Mexican fathers in Los Angeles, challenging segregation in schools in the Los Angeles area. Latinos eventually won that case in 1946 and on appeal in 1947. (Zehr, 2004) Latinos won another victory in *Keyes v. School District No. 1* (1973) against the Denver Public Schools which distinguished them as an identifiable class from African-Americans, although Brown served as support for their case. Finally, they benefited from *Lau v. Nichols* (1974) after a Chinese father sued to gain greater assistance for non-English speaking students to "be able to understand the curriculum." (Zehr, 2004) Thus, Latinos have had their own battle about desegregation, equity and language.

Blacks owe thanks to Latinos in California for their active involvement in the national struggle for equal education. In fact, it was Sylvia Menendez, not Linda Brown, who struck the first blow for school desegregation in California in 1944. (Munoz, 2004) Mexicans had fought for fair schooling opportunities for the children as early as 1930. (Munoz, 2004) Both Thurgood Marshall and

Justice Earl Warren, years before *Brown*, were involved in the *Menedez v. Westminster* case. Marshall filed a Friend of the Court Brief on behalf of the NAACP and Warren was governor of California (Munoz, 2004).

Sylvia Mendez and Linda Brown should both be commended, but Menedez was first. "While Brown was a major accomplishment . . . the Menedez case set the precedent that enabled Brown's attorneys to win their arguments before the Supreme Court." (Munoz, 2004) This reinforces my argument that Latinos and blacks must collaborate to achieve the illusory dream of equal education in America's public schools.

However, Hispanics are in a new and unique position as of the 2000 Census. They are now the largest minority in America, surpassing African-Americans. This means two things. They will exercise new political power and will be solicited more intensely for their votes. Also, they will be at the vanguard of confronting issues of discrimination. National entities such as *La Raza* already have a strong reputation for defending the rights of Hispanics.

It should be noted that Hispanics are struggling to be recognized as a diverse group. The majority of Americans tend to make the same mistake with Hispanics as was made with African-Americas. They are viewed as monolithic – that is, a single group with a single political ideology. However, this could not be more wrong. There is the commonality of language, but nuances of national heritage, culture and personal preference create a wonderful tapestry of diversity within the Hispanic community. Additionally, Spanish speakers can be found in every racial group. Hence, the politics and preferences of Hispanics or Latinos are hardly predictable. Black Hispanics are routinely overlooked altogether.

That being said, there are five major reasons why blacks and Hispanics should cooperate on the issue of public education. "To work effectively as an agent of change in a pluralistic society, it is necessary to connect with people different from oneself." (Tatum, 1997) First, there are more than 1 million Afro-Hispanics in America, many with ties to both communities. The economic profile of black Hispanics mirrors that of African-Americans. (Fears, 2003; Logan, 2003) Second, Hispanics have the highest dropout rate in public education, followed by African-Americans. Third, both groups depend heavily upon public education as a primary means of social and professional advancement. Therefore, blacks and Hispanics have ample reasons to work for better educational opportunities for future generations.

So, what can the two groups accomplish together? First, there can be a dialogue about the educational needs of minority children. It is important that the parameters of the problem be understood. The needs of the two groups are not identical but common ground exists. There are mutual problems of high dropout rates, overrepresentation in special education and under representation in gifted programs, excessive expulsions and suspensions and issues of teacher quality in schools with majority black and Hispanic populations. Additionally, there is the issue of residential isolation.

Second, black and Hispanic educators can explore new educational models such as smaller schools. Black and minority children need the reinforcement that smaller schools and class sizes allow. Factory-style schools are reservoirs for drugs, violence, social dysfunction and low academic performance. They also erode the sense of family that is a staple of black and Hispanic life in favor of the false sense of American independence. With greater opportunities for increased teacher contact in smaller schools, black and Hispanic students can be afforded the opportunity for higher academic achievement through stronger relationships with their teachers. A stronger student-teacher relation is essential to increased academic performance.

Third, blacks and Hispanics must work to bring together their considerable political clout to force legislative actions within their states to benefit public education. At the federal and state levels, public education tends to be under funded. Learning the lobbying process and becoming politically savvy is a necessary tool for bringing public resources to bear on community problems.

Public education is not an altruistic exception to politics. On the contrary, it is ineluctably tied to politics. Therefore, blacks and Hispanics must become more sophisticated in lobbying and other political tactics.

Fourth, and most important, blacks and Hispanics must build their own schools. Minorities must find ways to build schools that cater to the needs of the children within the neighborhoods where they live. The only way to get schools to mirror the values you want is to design and build the school yourself. How can this be done?

Education must become a high enough community priority that both groups are willing to seek private resources to build schools and hire highly qualified teachers and administrators to manage them. Building your own schools demonstrates a commitment. When whites want results, they build it. This is why a Ransom Everglades exists. Those parents invest in the institution. Here is a tactic worth duplicating.

The schools can be one of two kinds. The two groups can build either public charter schools or private schools. There are about 3,000 charter schools nationwide with California (500), Arizona (491), Florida (258) and Texas (241) leading the way. (Thorp, 2004) "Charter schools are publicly financed schools that operate largely independent of the regulations that govern most public schools." (Zehr, 2001) Generally, charter schools draw their students from nearby public schools, and attendance is voluntary. The advantage of charter schools is the access that parents, teachers and community leaders have in directly influencing curriculum choices. (Cannon, 2004) Charter school parents are essential in planning all aspects of the school, curriculum, mission, etc. Also, parents support the schools financially.

The schools are often born out of minority parents' frustration with public schools that make little effort to meet the special needs of their children. (Zehr, 2001) Unfortunately, the exasperation that leads to the founding of such schools often leads to poor planning in some cases. Hastily put together schools are often unsound at the outset. There is still some question as to whether charter schools are more effective in teaching children, partly because they are relatively new and partly because not enough time has elapsed for their performance to be studied longitudinally. (Zehr, 2001) However, they do eventually find their way.

The Lowell Community Charter School, some thirty-five miles north of Boston, is one such school. Its parents were frustrated with the violence between Cambodian and Hispanic youth within the public school system, and they were dissatisfied with the system's tepid response to the children's language needs. (Zehr, 2001) The parents felt this way even though the district had ". . . spent millions of dollars for staff development around issues of equity and education for English learners. . . ."

(Zehr, 2001) Lowell's make-up includes white and African American students.

Another point of interest with charter schools is that they are public schools run by a variety of entities (e.g., city governments, universities and colleges, and non-profit corporations). Charter schools receive their funding like public schools but must rely to some degree on the financial health of their parent organizations. In Florida, for example, parents can vote by majority to turn a public school into a charter school. However, the charter school can be placed at the mercy of public school boards if the operating body is not financially sound.

Another problem with charter schools is that there tends to be conflict between the governing body (i.e., the board) and the school site administration. This is not unusual since the governing board is usually learning its parameters in the early going. This can be overcome by hiring experienced administrators who have some knowledge of the local school system and some rapport with key stakeholders. This can make the transition smoother for both parents and children.

Still, the most important factor in the success of a charter school is its financial health. The school cannot just be the result of parental enthusiasm but poor organization and incompetent planning. The best intentions can be thwarted by such short-sightedness. The governing body must give priority to financial stability because the success of the school depends upon the school's ability to hire good teachers, administrators and to have adequate supplies. I have watched poor charter schools in Miami flounder under the economic strain.

Parental support is also indispensable to the success of charter schools. Public schools often suffer from blatant disinterest by parents. However, charter schools need parental support in order to meet the needs of students. Charter schools usually draw their students from nearby public schools; therefore, the problems can be the same. However, parents prefer the smaller class sizes and the personalized attention that charter schools offer.

Allow me to emphasize that parental involvement is what makes charter schools and private schools work. One of the major complaints of principals in inner city schools is that parents are not available. It will take schools that will be open on Saturdays and Sundays, if necessary, to capture those elusive parents. School must do the unconventional to serve the needs of minority children. This cannot always be done within the confines of a normal school day or a normal work week. Slight paradigm shifts often yield the best results.

Furthermore, parents cannot be absolved of their responsibility to take primary interest in the welfare of their children. Too often, minority parents – whether of necessity or neglect – abdicate the educational needs of their children to teachers and other adults rather than taking the lead. Successful education is accomplished when all the adults in a child's life share in the process. Villages don't raise children; people do.

In Miami, there has been abject silence at the decline of inner city schools. Schools that routinely field excellent sports teams make failing grades on the state assessments. Nearly every school that earned an "F" in 2003-04 on the state assessment was in a predominantly black or Hispanic community. More often than not, the principals were also black. As the governor announced gains, the failure of these schools were minimized because they, too, had made "gains."

At the same time, there was no outcry from parents. There were no hastily contrived town meetings -- nothing. Clearly, local and state officials did not care. Parents, not school administrators, need to take the lead in demanding that these schools be improved. It will not happen until parents make their presence felt. Why should a child have to leave his neighborhood to get a sound education when the school district has the responsibility of providing quality education in every school?

The other type of school minorities need to build are private schools. These schools are needed in order to develop and design the type of curriculum that includes the kind of spiritual and moral ideas that more affluent parents' desire. Private schools do not have to take everyone that applies. Also, the cost alone is prohibitive. Because of their financial security, private schools can be selective.

The cost of some private schools can be as high as college tuition, depending upon the school's reputation. Unlike public schools, private schools can choose the best students and reject less acceptable candidates. However, the benefit is that these schools usually offer strong college preparatory programs that connect well with first tier colleges and universities. The private school also offers parents the opportunity for greater participation. Minorities must have their private schools.

These kinds of schools are important. Public education is undergoing a transition. It is entering a new phase of existence. Charter schools, vouchers, and private schools are increasing the competition for students. Public schools are no longer able to rely on the luxury of receiving all the funding for themselves. Just as Catholic schools have used legal action to gain access to federal dollars, other kinds of private schools are coming into the education market.

Minority parents must have their schools. It is clear that minority children need their own role models. A recent study in Tennessee confirmed what many parents have feared. "Both black and white students score higher on mathematics and reading tests when their teachers are of the same race . . . ." (Viadero, 2001) This is an atrocity.

Nationally, minority children make up 40% of the students in public schools; however, only 13.5% of the teachers are minority.

As usual, students with a high poverty index show more deleterious effects from teacher related prejudice. "The race effects were particularly strong among poor children, children with inexperienced teachers, and children attending segregated schools – especially African-American children." (Viadero, 2001) *Let me add here that good teachers, regardless of their race or ethnicity or that of their students, produce successful students without "research-based programs." A good teacher can teach any child.*

The development of schools by and for minorities is essential to prevent minority children from being overwhelmed. When minority children are confronted with the American majority view of itself, they will encounter questions about their own identity. "The stereotypes, omissions, and distortions that reinforce notions of white superiority are breathed in by black children as well as whites. Simply as a function of being socialized in a Eurocentric culture, some black children may begin to value the role models, lifestyles, and images of beauty represented by the dominant group more highly then those of their own cultural group." (Tatum, 1997)

It is critical that minority students gain a sense of self and a sense of themselves within their cultural groups before the onslaught begins to erode their self-concept. They must know they are intelligent and capable because the time will come when that sense of self will be challenged. You cannot assume that white administrators will honor those ideals.

These institutions are also needed to counteract the ridiculous notion among school-aged children that being smart is anti-black. Prior to integration, blacks and minorities had a hunger to prove themselves against the assumptions of white Americans that they did not deserve to attend white schools at the public school or postsecondary level. Now, black and minority children criticize their peers for excelling. Minorities must have schools that acquaint children with the struggle for equal education and the continued quest for adequate resources in our communities.

Moreover, they must be taught that there are other role models who look like them. There is a whole new generation of black and Hispanic professionals and athletes who have set new standards. Their accomplishments are unimportant to America in general but are essential to building the self-confidence of minority students. For example, we now have black and Latino owners of major sports franchises in California and North Carolina.

Private schools for minorities can be successful. Schools such as those built by Dr. Marva Collins in Chicago (Westside Preparatory School) and Arthur Mitchell of the Dance Theater of Harlem (Manhattan School for Children) have demonstrated their benefit. Marva Collins' model has worked so well that is has begun to be franchised across the nation. Additionally, Collins has been asked to come into school districts and work with low-performing schools with astounding results. Her schools work because they duplicate age-old education principles of discipline and high expectations for students.

Also, these schools have reintroduced inner-city children to culture, refinement, foreign language and high academic achievement. The students from these schools graduate and attend college. These schools must be duplicated in every major city. These schools take the best of public and private schools and create environments where expectations are high and no excuses are given. Parents line up to get their children in these schools because the results speak for themselves. Children in these schools have high self-esteem and high achievement on both standardized tests and standard curricula.

Minority educators and communities must take up this challenge. Raise the money. We spend too much disposable income on temporary things that fade with time. We have the expertise to do this. There are black and Hispanic teachers and administrators who also need to take up this cause. Those who have retired know that so much more can be done but it must be done by the people, not the government.

The question presents itself here: where will the students come from? The answer is everywhere. Minority parents of all economic classes will send their children. They are frustrated with schools that rob their children of confidence and teach them nothing. Furthermore, the growing middle class includes minorities that can afford to pay for quality private education. Many are already sending their children to predominantly white schools despite the hostility that they sometimes meet there.

Minority parents want excellence, not excuses. Most would prefer minority private schools with integrated populations, not just because the students and teachers are black, but because the schools are good. Minorities have evolved beyond figureheads. They want real professionals with real skills.

I should have one final word here. These schools should be staffed by Master Teachers. Teachers like Jaime Escalante, Dr. Marva Collins, Arthur Mitchell, Salome Thomas-El, Hamid Ebrahim, Lou Yaniw, Septima Poinsette, Pat Sanders and their kind. (Hilliard, 2004) These are teachers and instructional leaders who inspire children to learn and defy the accepted philosophies that race, ethnicity and poverty affect outcomes. Their work demonstrates that good teachers trump socioeconomic and racial barriers.

Chapter Ten
The Swain Doctrine for Public Education

Having said all these things about the present state of public education, there is now something to propose about solutions. As much as I have criticized here the practices that limit the life possibilities of minority children, I would be remiss in not proffering some solution to these challenges. If I could design a school to service the needs of minority children, I would propose the following ten corrective actions:

1. If children are our most valuable resource, then the salaries of teachers must reflect our belief.

Teachers can be paid a deserving wage and these things should not be tied to incentives. The quintessential question here is where will the money come from? My answer is simple. If we can find $200 billion to steal oil from the Iraqi people, we can find as much for teachers in public education. The precedent has been set in such instances as increasing the number of law enforcement officers through federal dollars. The federal government also provided money to states and cities under the Clinton Administration for additional police officers to bolster the number of officers on the street. These precedents demonstrate that the federal government responds to priorities. The federal government created funds for 911 victims. We can find money when we need it.

Raising teacher salaries should be a national priority. While I understand the limit of federal authority under the 10th Amendment to the United States Constitution such that education remains under the authority of states, the federal government presently assists states to the tune of about 7% annually of their education budgets. The ability of America to compete on a global level is dependent upon succeeding generations of well-educated and competitive young people who will lead the country. To do this, we need the best teachers. In some case, the persons best qualified to teach core subjects in shortage areas such as mathematics and science are presently working in other fields. In order to lure those professionals, salaries must be commensurate.

We need our best minds working with children. There is a Biblical proverb that says *"As iron sharpeneth iron, so does a man sharpen the countenance of his friend."* The best make the best better. Our students need to be challenged throughout their educational careers. We need the best teachers at the elementary level to give our students a sound foundation. I have spent the last few years trying to convince a friend of mine who is perhaps the best teacher at her grade level to remain in this profession. However, the inability to be paid according to her efforts may cause her to either leave this system or to leave the profession all together. That is unfair for a person who gives her best for children. None of the arguments that I have heard so far counteract the dilemma of good teachers.

What is a teacher worth in America? Let me remind you. Teachers are entrusted with both the social and educational development of children. They are not responsible for the failures of legislatures who underfund public education. And then blame teachers for poor results. Public schools have to teach everyone who comes through the door --disruptive children, drug-addicted and drug-affected children, children who speak no English, children in mental and emotional distress, children with disabilities ranging from mild to severe and children who are unmotivated and, at times, unmanageable, disrespectful and violent. They also receive children who are not ready to learn at kindergarten and are asked to make them scholars. Public schools, due to legal mandates, do not have the luxury of selecting only the best students. They take what parents offer.

If children are truly important, then teacher pay must reflect that priority. Again, I am undaunted in this because the military budget in this country demonstrates that bombs rather than children are our priority. We need not be strong militarily and weak intellectually. Did anyone ever think for a minute that perhaps we missed the clues to 911 because maybe the best minds were not on the job? *Certainly we do not have the brightest mind sitting in the President's seat.* When I hear excuses like agencies simply did not communicate, I see a reason for better teacher pay. Our national security depends upon preparing our best minds.

2. Students must be trained at home to value school as an integral step toward their future living standard and earning power.

Teachers should not have to convince our children that education is important. The education of children is a community responsibility. The importance of education and its ability to improve one's station in life is not lost on the wealthy. They send their children to the choicest schools because they know that good preparation leads to better living conditions. The Ivy League tries to breed more Ivy Leaguers.

I spoke earlier of my visit to Ransom Everglades in the Coconut Grove area of Miami. When I walked through the campus, I felt better. I've been out of school for years. The sheer beauty of the place and the respect it commanded from me reinforced for me that parents saw this as a golden opportunity for their children. Children of poverty can be given this same appreciation for learning. Parents of minority children cannot leave school to chance. There is something to be said for emulating the tactics of the rich. They succeed because they demand quality.

Minority children must enter school with a zeal for learning. They must hunger for it. They must chase it. Education is fundamentally important but it is not a fundamental right under the Constitution. It is not because it is not mentioned there with "life, liberty and the pursuit of happiness." However, education is as important as breathing. It is a door out of misery for millions every year.

In my own case, my father went to the third grade. He was a construction worker. He could not vote until he was fifty. He had a heart attack when I was in the fourth grade and our middle class life spiraled down to a life of food stamps and government handouts. We became the family glad to receive the Thanksgiving basket.

The one legacy that my father gave me was he impressed upon me that teachers were in charge of the classroom; and I was there to learn, not to challenge them or tell them what to do. I went to school knowing that it was my chance. I went to school not caring about what other students were doing. *I was going to learn and excel.* I say this as a student who was good but never the best. I knew that teachers had what I needed. Good teachers like Howard Schutzman, who took me ice skating and taught me to play the trumpet; Ellen Heidt, who made me believe I could go to college; and Dr. Melvin Rahming and Dr. David Dorsey, who demanded excellence at the college and university levels.

I should add here that I came of age in school during the latter days of forced school desegregation. The books we received at Orchard Villa Elementary were never new. They were hand-me-downs from white schools. This was not a reason to fail. The knowledge might have been old, but it got me a *Phi Beta Kappa* key at Morehouse College. Knowledge from used books put me through graduate and professional school. To this day, I love learning because my father with the third grade education would not accept low grades and poor performance. By the way, the color of my teachers was irrelevant. I loved every one of them who loved me enough to teach!

3. *The atmosphere of school must be conducive to learning. Safety, high expectations, and clean schools are indispensable.*

Schools must be safe. This will never be accomplished with metal detectors. Safety comes from order. Schools must maintain an orderly environment. We have schools in Miami with more than 6,000 students. There are larger ones across the country. In such environments, everyone cannot have his own way. Catholic schools have uniforms and have worn them for generations. The effect of this is not just cosmetic. It helps them to know which children are theirs. It helps them to create an environment without envy over clothes.

Conversely, in the inner-city schools, students are attacking one another over designer clothing and failing school.

Moreover, the areas surrounding schools must be made safe. I know of at least one school in Liberty City, a predominantly black area of Miami, where students must navigate drug dealers and prostitutes to make it to the school door. Everyone knows this area is what it is. Yet, there is the danger of violence at every step. Children should not have to deal with that. The stakeholders in education must deal with this problem as much as any within the school building. Children do not come to school and forget what's just beyond the door. They are impacted by it. Are children important? Then, safety must be taken beyond the walls of the building.

Another aspect of safety must be the mental health of our students. In Miami, we agonized in 2004 over the death of a middle school student at the hands of a classmate who calmly committed murder in a bathroom and returned to class. Surely, there must have been some indicators, some red flags that foretold of this potential time bomb.

Did we not learn anything from Columbine? The two students who wreaked havoc on their classmates stocked weapons in their parents' garages. We must recognize that children are capable of the worst. But we must be able to detect this. Training is needed. The teacher is the first line of defense against such disasters.

4. *Schools must focus on customer service.*

The treatment that parents, students and community people receive in school buildings should rival that of a fine hotel. Every time I visit a hotel, I am reminded of the quality of service one receives from the car door to the counter and to the room. When was the last time you received this kind of treatment in a school? I have walked into school buildings and received some of the worst treatment of my life at the counter. We need to adopt the hotelier's model of service. If we are too busy to be nice to parents concerned about their children, perhaps we are too busy. Perhaps parents do not come to our buildings because they refuse to be overlooked.

How does a hotel, with lesser educated staff, manage to give better service? Simple: they train their staff to give the highest service possible regardless of the time of day. Their jobs depend upon it. Educators must begin to understand that their jobs are now competitive. Parents will seek other sources for the education of their children if we do not give the best service. Parents, students and the community are our customers. I have a suggestion. We should hire hotel staff to train school personnel in customer service.

When you arrive at a fine hotel, you are greeted at your car, escorted to the front desk and your questions are answered. You are escorted to your room and told to call if something is needed.

Also, when you call someone answers the telephone and provides that service in a matter of minutes.

Likewise, a school should greet parents, answer their questions and be as quick as possible about service. Schools sometimes have answering machines and no one answers the telephone directly. I cannot understand how this is possible in a public institution. If the public cannot contact us, we have absolutely failed the public.

People who work in the filed of public education are public servants. As much as the word *servants* may seem disparaging to some, it should not. School systems are governmental agencies that serve the needs of the public and school staff must be responsive to that. No company can stay in business that ignores the needs of the people it serves.

The question is: what do parents and students need most from us? First, they need our attention. Any principal who is too busy for parents is too busy. Second, they need clear communication in their home language. As the minority populations continue to grow within our country, we must produce documents that parents can read; and we must hire bilingual teachers and administrators. Bilingualism should become a part of teacher training. Third, our costumers need access to services. We must develop referral systems that are responsive to the vast health, emotional and spiritual needs of children and parents. Fourth, they would like us to smile while we serve them. No want wants service with a frown. People in the field of education remind me of going into a restaurant and being rushed by the waitress who never looks while taking my order. Good customer service requires that we be gracious.

5. *All teachers should hold a minimum of a masters degree and certification in their field.*

We cannot continue to hold students to high standards while holding teachers to minimum standards. A master degree should be earned within five years of initial employment. One does not become a doctor by sliding criteria. Doctors earn their credentials. Hence, they believe they are worthy of their pay. They never negotiate their fees. Lawyers are considered professionals. They are worthy of their hire. The professionalization of teaching cannot happen with minimalist standards.

If children are important then we should demand that teachers earn a masters degree in their teaching area within five years of employment. Working with pre-service teachers has convinced me that training above a bachelors degree is needed. You cannot raise certification standards and minimize the training that comes with a graduate degree.

Our students are no longer competing against the student next door. Competition for jobs in America is global. I made a call to my credit card company one day only to hear a voice with a very evident East Indian accept. I realized that the service calls had been outsourced and that my call was being answered by someone perhaps as far away as India. I am not provincial. I also understand that businesses make decisions based on the bottom line. But I also realized that India is presently a hotbed of technology. Therefore, I believe that our children must receive training from masters in their field if they are going to compete for increasingly scarce jobs.

This, too, reinforces my idea that teacher pay must increase. I suggest a national salary minimum for teachers of $100,000. If the number makes you cringe, then I ask: what are children worth? If they are precious, the people to whom we entrust them ought to be treated as if they were dealing with our most important asset. Teachers should not have to scrounge to pay their bills.

6. *We must invest in certified teachers and caretakers for students age 0-3.*

Brain research indicates that stimulation develops the synaptic pathways. There are certain activities that children need prior to entering pre-kindergarten to develop their readiness to learn. Children need activity. They need stimulation. They need an introduction to phonemic awareness. They need attention. This need can best be met by trained professionals.

One of the major complaints of kindergarten teachers is that the children entering school are not ready to learn. However, when is there ever dialogue between schools and the daycare centers in their immediate vicinity? The early learning experiences of children affect them for the rest of their lives. Schools and daycare centers must collaborate. How? Daycare center operators can spend the day with kindergarten professionals to learn some of the practical lessons that young people need to know. In education, there is the blame chart: high school teachers blame middle school teachers; middle school teachers blame elementary teachers; elementary teachers blame parents and daycare workers. Well, that's great for adults but terrible for children.

Again, research demonstrates that the development of synaptic pathways to develop in children under three years of age conditions the brain for learning. Hence, the most important learning experience in a child's life falls outside the purview of the public education system. What solution? Legislatures must begin to fund pre-school education in the truest sense of the word. Public education must begin to embrace the educational process that begins before pre-kindergarten. Even if only collaboratively, public schools must intervene in some way. It is the only way to improve readiness. None of the national initiatives such as Goals 2000, America 2000 provided funding for this.

7. We cannot continue to allow 40% of the student population to be exposed to inferior educational experiences.

Minority children exist in a parallel experience that prepares them for failure. Compulsory public education is a privilege, not a right. This is why inequity is allowed to exist. Racism and discrimination of other forms cannot be allowed to intrude into the educational system. While I acknowledge that they cannot be wholly excluded, we must be vigilant about it. When children in the worst school in the district receive the worst principal available and that school happens to be full of black children, it is not beyond the pale of truth that they are not valued. It simply could not happen in a white school. The parents would not tolerate it, and the school district would never consider it. A principal who earns two grades of "F" cannot stay in a school, regardless of his or her race or ethnicity. To leave that person there suggests that the children are not valuable.

Discrimination in any form is about one group believing itself more valuable than another. This is why I got hand-me-down books in elementary school. The school officials did not believe that children in Liberty City were important enough to deserve new books like their white peers across town. I attended a meeting at my old high school where the daughter of the first black superintendent stood up and begged for her child with special needs to receive services. In that same meeting, students asked: why can't we get full-time teachers? Why can't a child in a school graded "F" get a certified teacher?

Minority children have needs. The question is: are those needs important to school administrators and the legislators who fund schools? Poverty can be offset by good teaching. Disadvantages disappear when good learning takes place. The teachers I had were Jewish, white, Hispanic and black. Not one of them allowed me to take a day off. They insisted that I learned. I believe they cared about children. I never heard a single instance of a child questioning a teacher's racial or ethnic views. There were no slips of the tongue.

Schools are no different than the societies they serve. America is racist. Our schools are racist. That must change. Having black or minority figureheads does not negate racism. Racism happens at the highest administrative levels. I know black administrators in my school district who serve inordinate amounts of time as assistant principals and never get promoted despite repeated interviews.

At the same time, minimally qualified non-blacks are rapidly promoted. A very good teacher/media specialist left our school system after repeatedly making finals but never being selected to become an assistant principal. Other black administrators simply refuse to apply for jobs, fearing a fix. Others have grown tired of interviewing in vain.

Racism is stronger than discrimination because racism looks at color and uses power to limit life possibilities. When racism functions in school systems and prevents qualified black and minority administrators from advancing, it harms children. Moreover, we cannot allow children to be exposed to the least qualified and certified teachers and then blame them for an achievement gap. When Hispanic parents have to hold a hunger strike to get a new school for their children, I suspect something is amiss. This is discrimination pre-*Brown*. Children should not be exposed to separate and unequal education.

8. *Place the best administrators in the worst schools.*

I am not impressed by principals bragging about work accomplished in schools that would be successful no matter who is in charge. The best skills ought to be applied to the most difficult problems. I used to sit on school improvement committees to review the annual progress of schools in our regional offices along with regional administrators. I did this for about six years.

Invariably, principals from high performing schools, looking tanned and relaxed, would come into these meetings, sit back and let some assistant give the report. You could see that this person had not done a stitch of work. That school would have earned an "A" if Bugs Bunny was the principal. Yet, this kind of principal gets a reputation for success, having proved nothing. If these are truly the best principals who get the best results; then, the proper place for them is at the head of low-performing schools.

It is standard business practice to put resources where they are most needed. What school is more deserving of an experienced instructional leader than a low-performing school? I want to see principals who have the courage to volunteer for tough assignments. Is this politically incorrect? Again, are children important or is the reputation of the principal most important? If the children are important, then the best principals get the toughest assignments and time to perform the task.

Again, this is about customer service. The Baldridge and Sterling Education models come to mind here. Leadership is number one on each of these lists. Leadership is not just about the position, but how well that position communicates with and sets the tone for the organization. Schools need leaders who are innovative and daring. They must be able to communicate effectively what the mission of the organization is and how the staff members must go about developing and implementing goals.

Even though certain criteria are set by states and school districts, every school is different. There needs to be a unique approach taken in each building. Principals are often called upon to unseat cultures of failure and disharmony that have taken over buildings. Just as all teachers are not the same, all administrators are not specialists at turning around difficult schools. The core of the matter is that children deserve the principal who can get the job done.

9. Do not place principals in schools simply because they are black or minority.

I think most parents would prefer the best principal. It is both patronizing and naïve to present parents and students with a black principal, for example, just to play a color matching game. Just because the person is black does not mean the person is a good principal. Too many minority children have been subjected to this politically correct but damaging game. Figureheads are no good. The most important question in assigning administrators should be: can he or she accomplish the mission? Black and minority children need to do more than feel good. They need to be successful. They need high standards. They need principals who will put children first.

10. Rethink the school calendar. Our agrarian school calendar of summers off for students is outmoded.

Schools are too overcrowded, a condition that could be relieved by creating a rotating cycle of time on and off. Students can attend school year round and have sufficient time off by grouping them into cohorts. This would greatly relieve many of the issues of safety that tend to make schools unsuitable places for many children to learn. There is a marginal utility factor to crowding too many children of any age in one place. Populations of 6,000 to 8,000 students are common in large urban centers. School populations that exceed 3,000 students at the high school level are unworkable.

Neither can major cities build schools fast enough to keep up with burgeoning birth rights. Even if they could, there are problems to confront such as available space, the rising cost of land, safety and construction. Then, schools are often operating at capacity shortly after they are opened.

Moreover, students are often not capable of functioning in learning environments with thousands of peers and in classes with more than thirty five students. People tend to undervalue the marginal utility of large school buildings. There is a point at which too many students in one place defeats the purpose. Schools are beginning to look like industrial farms where thousands upon thousands of animals are forced to grow together. Children are not chickens and cows. They should not be warehoused.

If we were to change the school calendar to a year round model with students attending in shifts, we could relieve overcrowding and teachers could give children more individual attention. I concede that problems of students forgetting information during time off is possible, but I think this is outweighed by the practicality of reducing the phalanx that leads to frustration and violence.

Last Word

For the sake of preventing a misreading of this text, there are a few things that deserve reinforcement. First, race still is a major influence in American culture. There is this presumption when we discuss race that the sole objective is to offend. The American disposition of acting as if race problems do not exist and of railing against any mention of racial conflict prevents any real progress on the question. Just the mention of race creates dissent and elicits ravenous dislike. In fact, some people are offended at any issue regarding race. (Gutmann, 1996)

When it comes to public education, there is a real disparity in the quality of experience that minority and white children receive. Is it so heinous a question to ask why this systemic dysfunction persists? The outrage of those who benefit from this problem in public education has nothing to do with children. It has to do with fending off attempts by minority people to challenge the unearned privileges of the majority and demanding that the imbalance be corrected.

This attitude is not surprising. No one gives up privileges or power voluntarily. Lisa Delpit speaks of power as an exclusive club. Education offers access to that club. This is why no one rages against the open mistreatment of minorities. The simple truth is that the goal is to keep the entryway cluttered and deny access to as many a decency will allow.

So, while we fight wars against terrorism abroad, Americans of privilege engage in benign terrorism against minorities and against the poor. The mockery of black, Hispanic and poor white children matriculating through old, dilapidated schools and being exposed to second class teachers is its own form of warfare. It is warfare because it dooms countless millions to intractable poverty, leaves others open to the random violence of inner cities, and ushers some into the waiting arms of a criminal justice system built with the endless capacity of hell to enlarge itself daily.

People often ask: what do you want? I do not want Utopia. I want that minority children get a chance. For once, I would like the deck not to be stacked against those who start out with the least. I would like the parents of minority children to understand that there is still a struggle under way. Children cannot be left to caprice or happenstance. If those of us who have been privileged to gain some measure of success remain quiet in the face of injustice, who will speak for them?

The problem of the 21st century is the same as Dubois' problem of the 20th century. It is race, not class. It is the fact that people still view "others" as someone racially or ethnically different. It is the fact that policies continue to be promulgated to enlarge the powerful and debilitate the poor. America is a country that is skin deep. Our domestic and foreign policies demonstrate this daily.

A second issue of concern is America's idea of itself. We have not realized our potential. I want America to be the America I believed in as a boy. That America was always taking forward steps. I grew up in the generation of firsts. I believe one more first is due. We can be the first country to get fairness right. Constance Rice, the cousin of Condoleeza Rice, says, "Our system works for privileged kids of all races . . . My problem is that the public education system does not work for the majority of the children in it. And it is a devastating failure for poor kids of all races, including poor white children . . . We've got to break the mold." (Rice quoted by Wickham, 2004)

I want to begin this rebuilding process. Some things are not redeemable. They should be torn down and built from scratch. Our education system is tainted by racism. It cannot be fixed. New educational models must come onto the scene. New educational leaders must be found. New curriculum models must be launched. I challenge educators and parents to take the lead for change.

Bibliography

Appiah, K. Anthony and Amy Gutmann (1996). *Color Conscious: The Political Morality of Race*, Princeton University Press, Princeton, New Jersey.

"Basketball's Academic Fouls," (April 6, 2004). *USA Today,* p. 12A.

Black, Susan (December 2003). "Engaging the Disengaged," *American School Board Journal*, pp. 12-14.

Canon, Mark (May 10, 2004) "Charters Represent Finest Education," *USA Today*, p. 12A.

Chaddock, Gail Russell (August 18, 2003). "U.S. Notches World's Highest Incarceration Rate," *Christian Science Monitor*. www.csmonitor.com

Cook, Glen (December 2003). "Resegregation is on the Rise in the Shadow of Brown," *American School Board Journal*, pp. 12-13.

Darden, Edwin C. (December 2003). "The Race Challenge," *American School Board Journal,* pp.34-38.

Delpit, Lisa (1995). *Other People's Children: Cultural Conflict in the Classroom*, New Press, New York, New York.

Driscoll, Amy (May 16, 2004). "Civic Groups Combat Slave Trade," *The Miami Herald*, p. 1B

Dunn, Marvin (1997). *Black Miami in the Twentieth Century*, University of Florida Press, Gainesville, Florida.

"Equal Access to Schools Fails to Equalize Education," (April 29, 2004). *USA Today,* p. 11A.

Fears, Darryl (July 14, 2003). "Report Details How Race Affects Lives of Hispanics," *The Miami Herald*, p. 14A.

Garcia, Manny and Jason Grotto (January 26, 2004). "Odds Favor Whites for Plea Deals," *The Miami Herald*, p.1A.

Gates, Henry Louis and Cornel West (1997). *The Future of the Race*, Vintage Books, New York, New York.

Harrison, Paige and Allen J. Beck (2002). "Prisoners in 2001," *Bureau of Justice Statistics Bulletin*, pp. 1-16.

Hawes, Kay (November 6, 2000). "Getting in the Career Game," The NCAA News. www.ncaa.org/news

Haycock, Kati (December 2003). "Toward a Fair Distribution of Teacher Talent," *Educational Leadership,* pp. 11-15.

Hrabowski III, Freeman A. (January 2003). "Raising Minority Achievement in Science and Math," *Educational Leadership*, pp. 44-48.

Hilliard, Asa (April 4, 2002). *"Beneficial Educational Research: Assumptions, Paradigms, Definitions,"* A research paper presented to the American Educational Research Association, New Orleans, Louisiana.

Hilliard, Asa (April 2002). *"Assessment in a Multicultural Society [Assessment and Instructional Validity in a Culturally Plural World,"* A research paper presented to the American Educational Association Annual Meeting, National Council on Measurement in Education, Chicago, Illinois.

Hughes, Alan (March 2003). "A Brand New Game," *Black Enterprise Magazine,* pp. 105-109.

Kahlenberg, Richard D. (2001). *All Together Now: Creating Middle Class Schools Through*

Public School Choice, Brookings Institute Press, Washington, D.C.

Khetan, Sameer (May 31, 2004) "Philadelphia School District to Invest in Teacher Training," *The Daily Pennsylvanian,* p. 2.

Kohn, Alfie (1998). "Only for My Kids: How Privileged Parents Undermine School Reform," *Phi Delta Kappan.* pp. 569-577.

Kottak, Phillip (1991). *Anthropology: The Exploration of Human Diversity.* McGraw-Hill. New York, New York.

Krugman, Paul (2002). "For Richer: How the Permissive Capitalism of the Boom Destroyed American Equality," *The New York Times Magazine,* New York, New York, pp. 62-67, 76-77, 141.

Logan, John and Jacob Stowell and Dierdre Oakley (March 29, 2002). "Ethnic Diversity Grows: Neighborhood Integration Lags Behind," The Mumford Center.
www.albany.edu/mumford/census

Logan, John et.al. (December 18, 2001). "Ethnic Diversity Grows: Neighborhood Integration Lags Behind," The Mumford Center.
www.albany.edu/mumford/census

Logan, John et.al. (July 14, 2003). "How Race Count for Hispanics," The Mumford Center. www.albany.edu/mumford/census

Logan, John et.al. (October 13, 2002). "Separate and Unequal: The Neighborhood Gap for Blacks and Hispanics in Metropolitan America," The Mumford Center. www.albany.edu/mumford/census

Majaridge, Dale (December 1993). "Can We All Get Along," *Mother Jones*, pp.20-27.

"Major Cause of Joblessness Lies in U.S. Schools" (March 31, 2004). *USA Today.*

Matthews, Jay (March 3, 2001). "Black More Often Land in Special Ed, Report Finds," *The Miami Herald*, p. 21A. Matthews' article was based on a report by the Harvard Civil Rights Project. (www.law.harvard.edu/civilrights)

Munoz, Jr., Carlos (May 20, 2004). "Latinos Paved Way for Historic Case," *The Miami Herald*, p. 21A.

Nieto, Sonia M. (January 2003). "Profoundly Multicultural Questions, *Educational Leadership,* pp. 6-10.

Orfield, Gary (2001). Schools more Separate: Consequences of a Decade of Resegregation," The Harvard Civil Rights Project, pp. 1-49.

Orfield, Gary, Eric D. Frankenberg and Chungmei Lee (January 2003). "The Resurgence of School Segregation," *Educational Leadership*, pp.16-20.

Parenti, Christian (1999). *Lockdown America: Police and Prisons in the Age of Crisis*, Verso Books, New York, New York.

Patel, Joseph (2003). "Minority Report," *Vibe Magazine*, pp.124-132.

Pitts, Leonard (January 30, 2004). "Black Men, Stay Clear of Rigged Game of Justice," *Miami Herald*, p. 1B.

Powell, John A. (October 1999). "Achieving Racial Justice: What's Sprawl Got to Do With It," Poverty and Race, Vol. 8, No. 5, www1.umn.edu/irp/announce/PRRAC1999.htm.

Relin, David Oliver (April 4, 2004). "Won't You Help Feed Them," *Parade Magazine,* pp. 6-9.

Rightmire, Phillip G. (2003). "160,000 Year Old Skulls Found," *USA Today*.

Robinson, Randall (2000). *The Debt: What America Owes to Blacks*, Plume, New York, New York.

Robinson, Randall (2004). *Quitting America: The Departure of a Black Man From His Native Land*, Dutton, New York, New York.

Rolon, Carmen (January 2003). "Educating Latino Students," *Educational Leadership*, pp. 40-43.

Sage, George H. (1990). *Power and Ideology in American Sport: A Critical Perspective.* Human Kinetics Publishers, Champagne, Illinois.

Sorhaindo, Linda (2003). "The Relationship Between Poverty and Student Achievement," Doctoral Dissertation, University of Miami, School of Education, Coral Gables, Florida.

Steele, Shelby (November 2002). "The Age of White Guilt and the Disappearance of the Black Individual," *Harper's Magazine*, pp.33-41.

Swartz, Jon (July 6, 2004) "Inmates vs. Outsourcing", *USA Today* Online. http://www.usatoday.com/omney/economy/employment/2004-07-06-call-center_x.htm.

Tatum, Beverly Daniel (1997). *Why Are All the Black Kids Sitting Together in the Cafeteria?* Basic Book, New York, New York.

Thorp, Peter (May 10, 2004) "Faulty Program is Exception, *USA Today*, p. 12A.

"Thousands of New York Students Expected to Repeat 3rd Grade," (June 4, 2004). *USA Today*. www.usatoday.com/news/education/2004-06-04-3rdgraders-fail_x.htm.

"The Chronic Underrepresentation of African-Americans in Medicine," (Winter 2004). *ETS Policy Notes,* Vol. 12, No. 1, Princeton, New Jersey.

U.S. Department of Justice (2003). "Education and Correction Populations," Bureau of Justice Statistics. www.ojp.usdoj.gov

Vail, Kathleen (December 2003). "The Social Challenge," *American School Board Journal,* pp.46-52.

Viadero, Debra (September 12, 2001). "Teachers' Race Linked to Students' Scores," Education Week on the Web. www.edweek.com/ew/newstory.cfm.

Wells, Spencer (2002) *The Journey of Man: A Genetic Odyssey,* Random House, New York.

Wickham, Dewayne (September 8, 2003). "Race Trumps Schooling," *USA Today.* www.usatoday.com.

Wickham, Dewayne (May18, 2004). "Rice's Cousin Determined to Rebuild Our Schools," *USA Today*, p. 21A.

Wise, Tim, (February 20, 2003). "Whites Swim in Racial Preference," *AlterNet.org.* www.alternet.org.

Witzig, Ritchie (October 1996). "The Medicalization of Race: "Scientific Legitimization of a Flawed Social Social Construct," *Annals of Internal Medicine.* Vol. 125, pp. 675-679.

Wooten (December 28, 2003). "Race Reversal: Man Lives as black for 50 Years – Then Finds Out He's Probably Not," *ABC.com.* www.abcnews.com/sections/nightline/sciTech

Zehr, Mary Ann (September 12, 2001). "One School, Two Cultures," *Education Week on the Web.*
www.edweek.com/ew/newstory.cfm.

Zehr, Mary Ann (March 10, 2004). "Close to Home," *Education Week*, Vol. 23, No.26, pp. 33-34.

Zehr, Mary Ann (March 10, 2004). "A Long Struggle for Equality," *Education Week*, Vol. 23, No.26, p. 34.